Fa

MW00907850

Video Editing

M. Beygirci

DATA BECKER®

Copyright © 2002 by   DATA BECKER GmbH & Co. KG
                       Merowingerstr. 30
                       40223 Düsseldorf

Copyright © 2002 by   DATA BECKER CORP
                       154 Wells Avenue
                       Newton
                       MA 02459

Published by   DATA BECKER CORP
                       154 Wells Avenue
                       Newton
                       MA 02459

Author   Muzaffer Beygirci

Printed in the United States   May 2002

UPC CODE   6-80466-90212-6

ISBN #   1-58507-117-X

DATABECKER® is a registered trademark no. 2 017 966

Contents

Introduction

Your best friends just returned from their vacation, and they invite you over to view their vacation videos. You are panic-stricken because you still remember the vacation videos from last year: a seemingly endless evening with hours and hours of video material; most of it was blurred or it zoomed inway too fast with the worst accompanying commentary ever and constant fast-forwarding ...

Now imagine your friends showing you a short video with a pictoral landscape, wonderful weather, nice people, and the funny adventures they had. You would want to go on that vacation yourself and probably wouldn't mind seeing more vacation videos in the future, wouldn't you?

This book is intended to show you that video editing is not only reserved for the pros. Anybody owning a standard PC, a video camera, and a suitable video card can become a director and cutter. Since ME & XP, the cutting software is even provided with the operating systems: Windows Movie Maker, the software chosen as the foundation of this book.

Capturing and optimizing videos

Before you can start editing your video, you must transfer your video data to your PC. This process is called *capturing* and is no different from *recording*. During this procedure, a digital copy of your videotape is transmitted onto the hard disk of your computer. Therefore, capturing is also frequently called *digitizing*. The original remains unmodified during this procedure.

There are basically two different ways of *digitizing* videotapes: you can either digitize the entire movie at once or capture individual scenes.

Individual scenes or everything at once?

It is advisable to capture videos in individual scenes. This way you can prevent hard disk capacity problems and save yourself time because there is no need to take the captured clip apart into individual scenes later on. This method also facilitates the management of the clips.

Before you get started

Once Windows XP is up and running, connect your camcorder to your PC by way of the FireWire cable and turn it on afterwards. Windows identifies your camcorder as a new device and notifies you about it as follows:

You can see on the bottom left that a *Canon DV Camcorder* was found. Of course this information might be different, depending on the device you are using.

9

1. Capturing and optimizing videos

If the camcorder is not recognized properly

Usually, Windows XP recognizes all camcorders properly. It is possible that Windows might not recognize your camcorder if you are using a brand new model. In this case, you are notified that a camcorder was found (without the proper designation). Nearly 99% of the time you can continue working without any problems if no camcorder was recognized. Please contact the manufacturer of your video camera if you still have problems because it can help you and offer any available driver updates.

Afterwards, Windows announces itself once more:

Select *Take no action* and check off the option *Always do the selected action*. Otherwise, this message appears every time you plug your camcorder into your PC. In case you are working with different video editing software later on, it might be annoying if Movie Maker is started automatically each time the camcorder is turned on. If, on the other hand, you always want to work with Movie Maker, you can select the option *Record video using Windows Movie Maker* and click *OK* afterwards.

Starting Windows Movie Maker

You can now start Movie Maker using the Windows Start menu: *Start/All Programs/ Accessories/Windows Movie Maker*.

On the left side, notice the collections, which, of course, are still empty. More collections appear once you have digitized a number of videos. A short preview of each video is then displayed in the window in the middle.

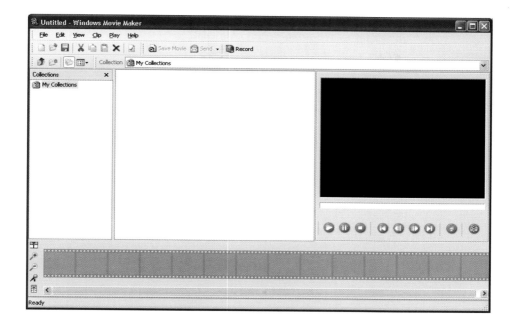

To the right, you can find the preview window. The actual video is displayed here. It doesn't make a difference whether it is played directly from your camcorder or whether the files are located on your hard disk.

Preparing for video capture from your camcorder

To start the video capture (digitization), click the *Record* button:

The *Record* window opens displaying the presets and the current video image, which is provided by the camcorder.

You can find different setting options on the left side:

1. Capturing and optimizing videos

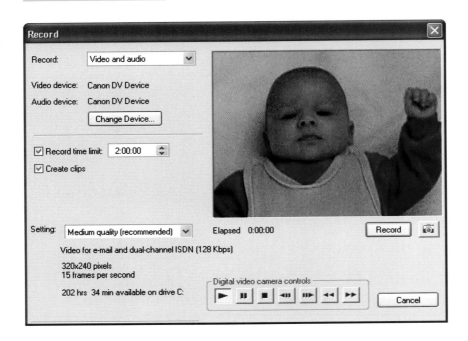

- *Record:* You can choose whether you want to record video and audio, audio only or video only.

- *Video device:* Specifies the device that is used to record video data.

- *Audio device:* Indicates the device that is used to record audio data.

- *Change Device:* In case your PC contains a number of video and audio sources, you can select them here (for example, USB camera, video/graphics card with Video In or TV card).

- *Record time limit:* You can specify here whether the recording should have a time limit. Once the predefined time has elapsed, the recording stops automatically.

- *Create clips:* This is a special function that you can choose to enable the program's automatic scene recognition. Movie Maker then automatically creates a separate clip for each scene.

- *Setting:* Here, you can define the quality of the videos to be recorded.

Video quality settings

You must change a number of settings before you can work with your camcorder:

1 Switch your camcorder to Playback mode (also called VCR mode).

2 Disable the option *Record time limit* (this way you are not limited by a pre-defined recording time). Then select *Setting/Other...* as well as *DV-AVI (25 Mbps)* from the list that appears.

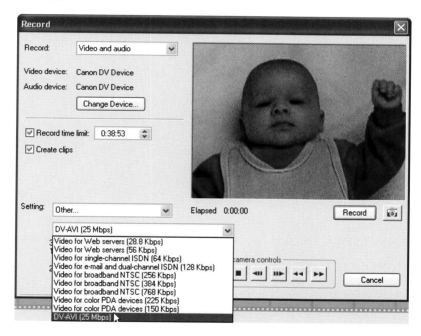

Attention camera rolling!

Now that the preparations are finished, you can start the capturing of your videos.

1 Start the playback of your camcorder.

1. Capturing and optimizing videos

Camera controls

Most camcorders can be controlled through the recording software, that is, you don't necessarily need to start the playback of your camcorder manually. A simple click on the *Record* button is sufficient.

The video camera control bar only appears in Movie Maker if you are using a digital camera. With all other video sources, this control bar does not appear.

Use the buttons as follows (from left to right):

Playback, Pause, Stop, Skip Back, Skip Forward, Rewind, Fast Forward.

2 Now click *Record* (without starting the camcorder beforehand, if you are using a digital camcorder). [Record]

3 Below the preview window, which dis- plays the current video image, the elapsed

| Elapsed 00:00:02 | Recording | [Stop] | 📷 |

recording time is displayed. Next to it, the message *Recording* is blinking, indicating that the recording process has been started.

4 After you have recorded the desired scene, click *Stop*. Optionally, you can also press (Esc).

If your camcorder can be controlled with the software, it should have stopped automatically. If this is not the case, you must stop your camera manually.

Using your TV as a control monitor

Most camcorders have a video output that runs parallel to the FireWire output. This enables you to connect your camcorder to your TV; consequently, you don't have to rely on the small preview window of Movie Maker.

In addition, you PC monitor might modify the video image. Colors, contrast, and luminosity of the original might not be displayed correctly. For this reason, professionals work with *video monitors* that provide a significantly better picture than regular TVs. The camcorder image appears exactly the way it is leaving the camera. For the amateur video editor, the TV works as an excellent supplemental monitor to the PC monitor.

5 Your video was transferred to your PC. The *Save Windows Media File* window is now open; you must choose a file name for the recorded scene and select the file destination on your hard disk.

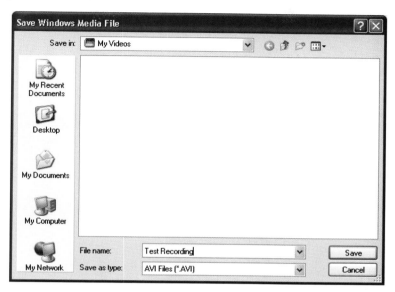

Assign a name to your video and click *Save* afterwards. A dialog window opens that displays the current status of the saving process:

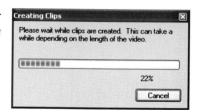

Once the saving has stopped, the following message box appears:

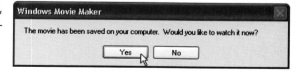

Click *Yes* to view the recorded clip.

1. Capturing and optimizing videos

Trust is good; control is better

You should always use this playback function to evaluate whether your clip has been successful. This saves you a lot of work in case an error occurred in your recording. Take your time and watch the video closely. If the desired scene was not captured fully, you can delete the file and start the recording anew.

Windows Media Player then opens automatically, and the video plays back:

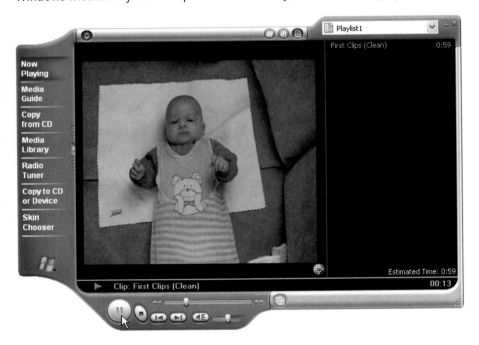

You have recorded your first scene. Click *Record* again to digitize further clips. This way you can transfer all scenes bit by bit to your computer. The presets you defined in Movie Maker remain saved, that is, you don't have to redefine all settings (format, resolution and quality).

To cut your video later on, all scenes of the video have to be on your hard disk in *digitized* format.

Material without boundaries

It is not necessarily worthwhile to transfer as much video material as possible to your PC. Even pros use only a small portion of their extensive material in the final production. You should make sure that you choose a good selection of scenes to be used in the video before actually digitizing them. Please take into consideration that the editing of digital video accumulates large quantities of data : approximately 3.7 MB for 1 second of video material. That means a video clip that is one minute long takes up about 220 MB. You don't need to be too critical when it comes to capturing videos, however. It doesn't matter if you recorded a few scenes too many or recorded them incorrectly because they can be deleted at any time – this way hard disk space can be freed up again.

Scene recognition

The scene recognition feature of Movie Maker splits the recorded video into its individual scenes.

This automatic function greatly facilitates your work. However, you won't necessarily want to leave it up to your computer to decide which part belongs to a scene and which one doesn't. For this reason, you should always record individual scenes. It doesn't matter if the scene contains images at the beginning and at the end that are not part of it, as scenes can be cut precisely later on and undesirable images can be removed this way.

To disable the scene recognition function of Movie Maker, you must go to *View*, select *Options*, and remove the checkmark in front of *Automatically create clips*.

Capturing other video sources

You can use all of the video sources in Movie Maker that are supported by your PC. You could use grabber cards, graphics cards with a Video In, TV cards or USB cameras, for instance. The latter have become popular lately because they can be acquired inexpensively. They are also perfect for video chats such as Netmeeting or CuseeMe. This way you can see the person you are chatting with (provided that the person at the other end also uses a camera), and if you also own a microphone, you can also hear your chat partner.

Setting up a USB camera

1 Connect the USB camera to your computer and start Movie Maker. If you are using a different video source (such as a TV card, for instance), connect the video input device and turn it on. This could be a VCR or the antenna cable for your TV card.

2 Click *Record*.

         [Record]

3 Select the option *Change Device* from the Record dialog window; then select your video device from the menu. Click *OK* to confirm your selection.

Depending on the video device you are using, the dialog window on your screen might contain different entries.

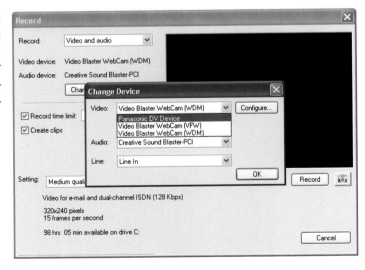

Note

Driver models

You can choose between VFW and WDM. You should always use the WDM entry (WDM stands for **W**indows **D**irect **M**edia). This is a new driver model that was developed to remedy the problems of the previous VFW (**V**ideo **f**or **W**indows) version. Video for Windows drivers are usually only provided for compatibility reasons. Before you start your recording, you should check on the Web site of the manufacturer of your camera or TV card to learn if a more current driver is available than the one you are using.

4 Select the option *Other* under *Setting*.

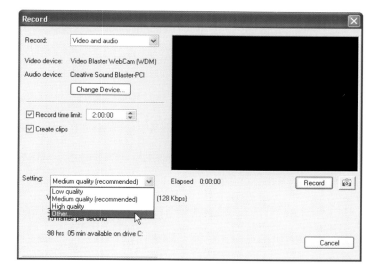

5 Select the speed of your Internet connection from the following list:

1. Capturing and optimizing videos

Defining data rate

You should repeat the following step at different settings later on to obtain the optimum data rate settings. It's best to start with *Video for single-channel ISDN* this time. When you carry out your next attempt, you can choose the next entry. Please remember to assign specific names to your clips when saving them later on. This way you know later on which settings you used (for instance: test_video1_64Kbps).

6 Record your video by clicking *Record*.

[Record]

There might be no preview image displayed during the capture of your video. The device driver you are using might cause this. Nowadays, hardly any TV cards do not support *Overlay mode*. In *Overlay mode*, the video data is bypassing the processor and directly written into the video memory. This doesn't put any strain on the processor, and the video is displayed smoothly on the monitor screen.

7 Stop your recording by pressing [Esc] or by clicking *Stop*.

[Stop]

8 The Save dialog window opens.

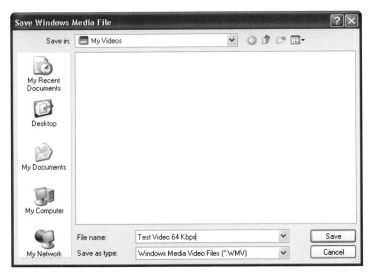

9 Enter a file name and click *Save*. The captured video is saved as a WMV file (Windows Media Video).

Note

Automatic capturing

Advanced video editing systems that usually contain an additional capture card, offer the *Batch Capturing* function. This function allows you to set the exact mark-in and mark-out points before the video is actually digitized. These points indicate when the recording should be started and when it should be stopped again. Once you have let the program know which scenes you want to capture (frame-specific), you can click Record. The capture software then automatically rewinds the videotape and starts to record the corresponding scenes by itself.

Compiling the first video

As with TV images, the individual images in a camcorder are played back so fast that the human eye cannot make out their individuality. A succession of individual images becomes a fluid video image. For the NTSC standard, these are 29.97 frames per second, each frame consisting of two half-frames. This allows an even better playback of the video.

With digital video, the frames aren't strung one after the other as they are with Super8, but are saved in digital form on the magnetic data carrier of the videocassette.

When editing digital video, you must go through several steps until the video is done. The steps start with the digitizing, as you have already found out. Afterwards, you need to edit the recorded clips. This is where you need to use editing software like *Windows Movie Maker*.

Working with the storyboard

The term storyboard describes a work and planning process in which you sketch the sequence of the video. On the storyboard, you determine the order of the scenes, nothing more.

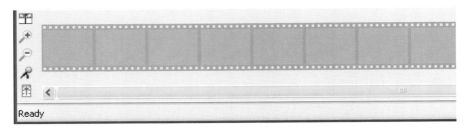

Because you are doing non-linear video editing here (the scenes are not strung one after another on the video tape), you can access any scene at any time and can change the succession of the clips as desired.

Storyboard or timeline?

In principle, all video editing programs work in similar ways. Most programs come either with a timeline or a storyboard, or a unified version of both. Depending on the task, the one or the other option might be more convenient. For assembling a basic sequence, a storyboard is always good. For detail work on the video sequence, a timeline is better.

1 Open Movie Maker.

In the center window you can see the captured clips. This allows you to decide which scene you want to use when.

Look at the clips again

If you're not sure about the content of your clips anymore, select one of the thumbnails in the center window. Each thumbnail represents the first frame of each scene. Then press *Play* located on the taskbar in the preview window and watch the clip.

2. Compiling the first video

2 Click the first video sequence and drag it to the storyboard. The sequence then appears in the first field of the video track on the storyboard.

3 Drag the following clips one by one onto the storyboard in the same way. You should now have a similar view (the images depend on the clips you used, of course).

4 To change the sequence, click a clip and drag it to the position where you want it while pressing the mouse button. This way, you can move the fourth clip into the second position, for instance: click the fourth clip and drag it to the left until the gray bar appears between Clip1 and Clip2.

5 Now release the mouse. The clip that used to be last is now in the second position.

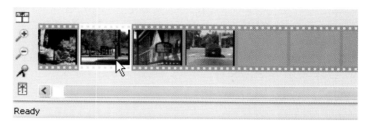

Of course, it is also possible to drag the clip from the selection in the center to the correct position and delete the one that was mistakenly placed.

Removing clips from the storyboard

You can delete a clip from the storyboard by right-clicking it, then selecting the *Delete* command from the pop-up menu. Optionally, you can select a clip with the mouse and then press Delete.

Note

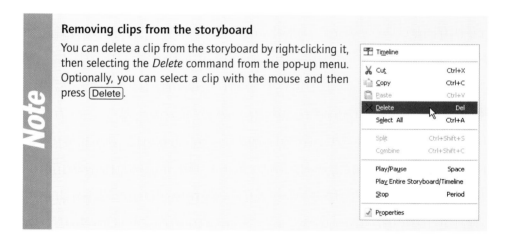

6 To play back the clip, right-click the storyboard and select the command *Play Entire Storyboard/Timeline* from the pop-up menu.

7 Now go to the preview window and click *Play*.

Watching an individual clip

If you don't choose the *Play Entire Storyboard/Timeline* command from the pop-up menu, only the selected clip plays back.

The captured scenes are now on the storyboard. Because you cannot capture too accurately with Movie Maker, you need to crop the scenes afterwards.

Cutting scenes to the right size

You can cut a scene to the right size either on the storyboard or directly on the timeline.

On the storyboard

1 Start Movie Maker and import a clip onto the storyboard.

2 Go to the preview window on the right. Drag the small triangular slider to the point where the extra footage begins.

If you cannot hit the exact spot with the slider, you can use the *Next* and *Previous Frame* buttons. Every time you click one of these buttons, the following/previous frame is shown.

3 Hover over the small triangle of the slider while pressing the right mouse button. When the *Split* message appears, click it.

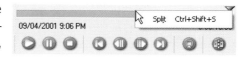

This splits the first area of the clip from the latter so that the undesired footage appears as an additional clip on the storyboard.

4 To delete the second clip from the storyboard, right-click it; then select the *Delete* command from the pop-up menu. You have just edited your first scene.

If the undesired frames are located at the beginning of a scene, you can proceed in the same way as above, with the exception that you are deleting the first clip resulting from the split (the cut area). To do so, move the slider in the preview window to the position in the clip where the area to be cut off ends.

Then right-click the slider and choose the *Split* command. Now the clip is split into two, and you can delete its first part.

On the timeline

You can also trim clips on the timeline. Unlike on the storyboard, here you have more options for manipulating the scenes.

1 Start Movie Maker and import a clip onto the storyboard.

2. Compiling the first video

2 Click *Timeline* to switch to the timeline mode.

3 At the bottom left you can see two small triangles above the filmstrip. These are the markers for the beginning and the end of the scene.

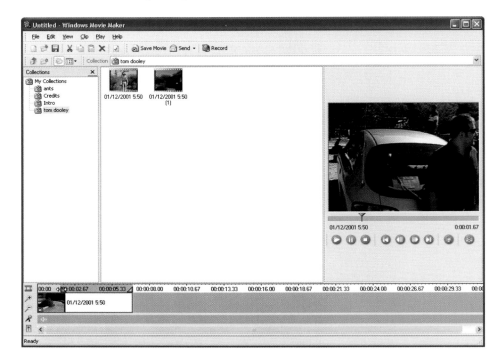

Move these markers to trim the scene. Click the left triangle and drag it to the left past the undesired parts. Simultaneously, you can see the current video frame in the preview window. Now release the mouse button.

As a result, the scene on the timeline is trimmed according to where you set the marker. Proceed in the same manner with the end of the clip, if you want to trim it as well.

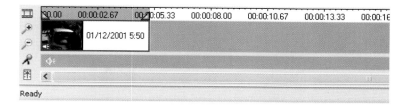

Note

Navigating the clip on the timeline more easily

If you have difficulty getting to a particular frame on the timeline, click the magnifier icon to "zoom in" on the time division.

Inserting transitions between scenes

Until now you have lined up the clips on the storyboard. In the completed video, the scenes would be played back without any transition effects. As long as you want to create a fast and easy video that doesn't need any dissolves, you can work on the storyboard, where things aren't very complicated. Line up the clips one after the other, so that the scenes are separated by hard cuts.

Such videos are rather boring, however: you can achieve the same effect by playing the video directly from the camcorder. To add interest to your video, you should insert transitional elements between the individual scenes. They not only make the video more exciting but also allow the viewer to prepare for each new scene.

Abrupt interruptions disturb the viewer; the transitions between scenes should be soft. Dissolves are an excellent way of making the video flow. If you use strenuous effects, on the other hand, the idea might backfire.

Transition effects

Most video editing programs offer a wealth of transition effects (dissolves).

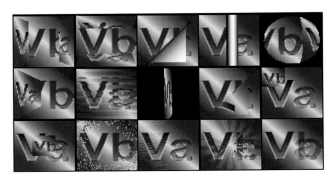

The options for the transition elements allow you to further modify them, so you can soon have hundreds of possibilities for bridging scenes at your disposal. In addition, some manufacturers of special-effects software have specialized in such dissolves, and you can buy add-ons for your video-editing software. However, make sure to first ask the manufacturer of the special-effects software whether your video-editing program supports the effects. Not all dissolves can be used with all video-editing programs. But before you start hunting for new effects, try out the ones at your disposal. Even professionals don't normally work with more than three or four transition effects.

In Movie Maker, you have two kinds of transitions at your disposal: a hard transition (which you already know) and a soft transition. During the latter, the two video sequences overlap and slowly dissolve from one into the other.

Inserting soft transitions

To work with soft transitions, you need to switch to the timeline mode.

1 Start Movie Maker, and then switch to timeline mode by clicking *Timeline* at the bottom left of the storyboard.

2 Import two clips onto the timeline. To do so, drag two scenes from *My Collections* to the timeline, while pressing the mouse button.

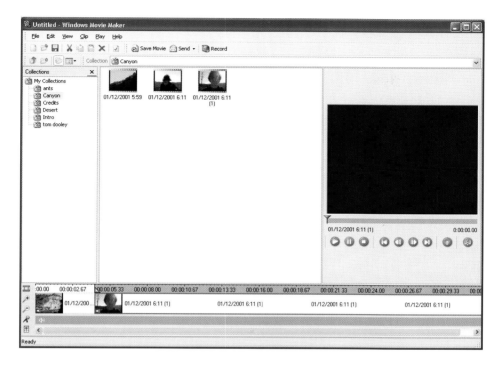

3 Click the icon showing a magnifying glass with a plus twice to increase the resolution of the timeline.

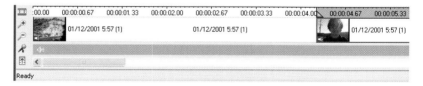

4 Now click the second video and drag it a little over the first.

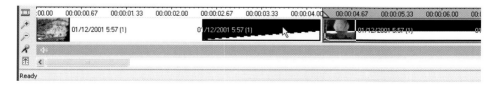

2. Compiling the first video

While you are dragging the second clip, look at the black-and-white area to make out the duration of the transition. Keep the duration of the transition to a minimum: it shouldn't be any longer than three seconds, but it also shouldn't be any shorter than one second.

5 After you release the mouse button, the transition area appears dark gray:

Right-click the timeline and select the command *Play Entire Storyboard/Timeline* from the pop-up menu. In the preview window, click *Play*.

The transition in our example looks like this: The last frame *before* the dissolve ...

The frame in the middle *during* the dissolve ...

The first frame *after* the dissolve.

Titles that capture the imagination

Every time you watch a movie or documentary on television, the opening scene has a title, also called the opening credits. These can be quite plain or rather complex using, for example, animated three-dimensional text.

With home videos, too, the title should be present at the beginning of the movie and it should match the content.

Later on, you learn how to create titles using the tools in Microsoft's *Paint* application and how to embed them in Movie Maker.

Creating titles using Paint

Microsoft's Paint application is a graphics program and has been a standard component of the Windows group of operating systems since the release of Windows 95. The application is basic but totally adequate for the purpose of creating a title.

Tip

Interesting opening credits

The opening credits should be appealing to your audience and awaken their curiosity. Avoid using multiple fonts and font sizes, because you may lose your viewers' focus. If possible, refrain from using small fonts as these can become blurred and possibly illegible when viewed in your movie later on. Make sure that the opening credits match the movie's contents: After all, they are advertising your movie!

Note

NTSC Systems (for example, USA, Japan)

Please ensure that you adjust the size of the image according to the local resolution. In countries using the NTSC system, the resolution is 720x480 pixels instead of 720x576 pixels, as in countries using PAL.

1 Run *Paint* by going to *Start/Programs/Accessories/Paint*.

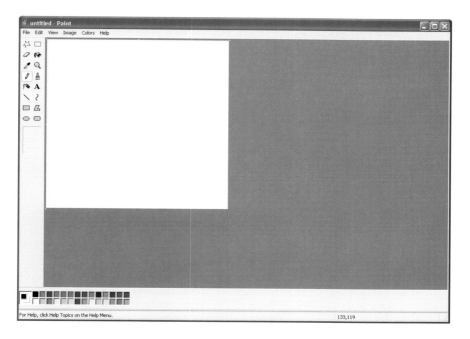

2 First of all, set the appropriate size of the image. Select *Image/Attributes* from the menu bar.

3 Because the United States uses NTSC resolution, you must select a width of 720 and a height of 480 pixels. Please change the settings accordingly should centimeters or inches be shown rather than pixels. Confirm your selection by clicking *OK*. You have now established the basis for creating the title.

4 The first step is to fill the white background with color. Select *Fill With* *Color* in the toolbox on the left side of the screen. The pointer changes to a small bucket with paint pouring out.

Activate the background color by clicking 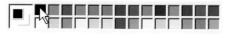 the appropriate color in the color boxat the bottom left corner of the window. If pos- sible, choose colors that compliment the content of the video. For example, use yellow for a movie that begins in a desert. Black is usually a good option.

35

3. Titles that capture the imagination

Once you have selected your chosen color, click your mouse inside the white area of the image.

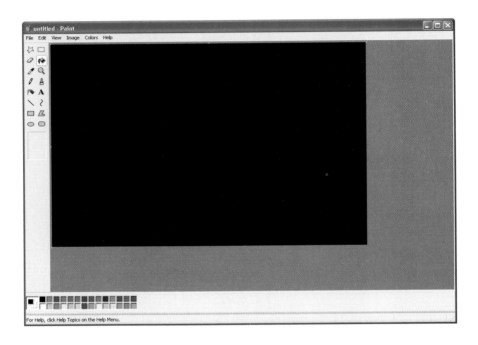

Just like at the movies

Most movies open with a black screen. You might choose to use this approach when first launching your movie. To do so, create an empty, black image containing no text. Not displaying the credits right away has a much bigger impact. Save the image using a meaningful name, such as *Credits1*. Go to *File/Save As* on the menu bar and select *24 Bit Bitmap(*.bmp;*.dib)* in the subsequent menu under *Save as type*. Use this image later on during the opening and closing credits.

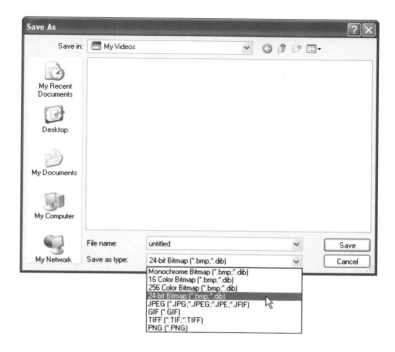

5 To insert text, click the *Text* icon and drag the pointer to create a text box of the size you require.

Additional fonts

Use any fonts currently installed on your system. In case these do not meet your require-ments, you can download additional fonts from the Internet. The easiest way to do this is to enter the term *Fonts* into a search engine on your Web browser. Countless versions of free fonts are available through the Internet. Once you have downloaded the appro-priate fonts, all just copy them into the *C:/Windows/Fonts* directory.

To adjust the font and font size, place the pointer inside the text box and right-click your mouse. Activate *Text Toolbar* in case this option is not currently checked.

3. Titles that capture the imagination

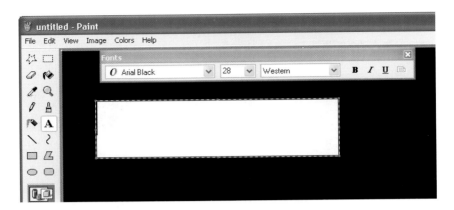

6 Insert the required text into the text box that you have just created; then click another area in the window to exit the text box.

It is possible to change the font, font size, and forecolor at any time while you are still editing the text. If you are not sure yet which font to use, you can type the text first and then try out the various fonts by selecting them from the Fonts menu.

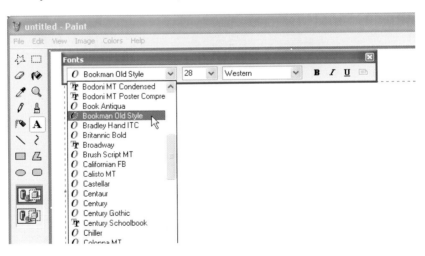

7 In the following example, not all sections were filled in:

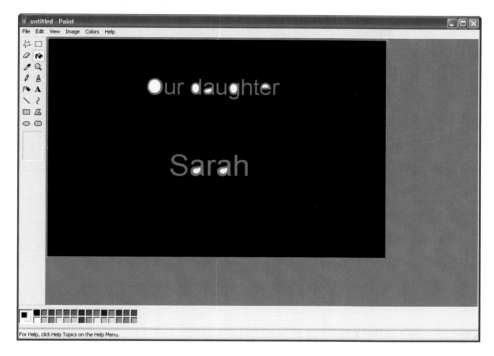

Click the paint bucket and select the chosen background color from the color box. Click your mouse inside the areas that have not yet been colored in (in our example these are the areas inside the letters e, o, and a).

8 Finally, save the image. Go to *File/Save* and select *Save as type: 24 Bit Bitmap* in the subsequent Save As window. You can now exit *Paint*.

Inserting the opening credits into your video

To create the opening credits in Movie Maker, you must import the images that you created in Paint into the collection first.

3. Titles that capture the imagination

1 Activate Movie Maker. Right-click your mouse inside the field *My Collections* on the left side and select *Import* from within the pop-up menu.

2 From within the subsequent file selection window, locate the image that you created in Paint. In case you created multiple images, repeat these steps.

3 Select the image icon and drag it into the first clip in the Storyboard.

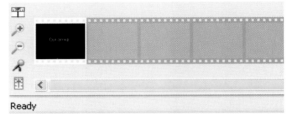

4 Switch from Storyboard to Timeline mode by clicking the Timeline icon and select the playback duration.

5 In the top right corner of the image, notice a small triangle. Hold the mouse over the triangle to change the shape of the cursor to a double-sided arrow. Press and hold the left mouse button.

This enables you to adjust the playback duration. Drag the mouse to the right to increase the duration. Drag the mouse to the left to decrease it. To get an idea of the real time duration, check the seconds display in the monitor.

If you release the mouse near the seven-second mark, the opening credits appear for seven seconds. Follow this procedure to insert images into your video at any point.

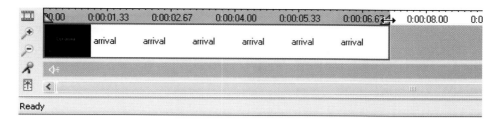

6 You can now insert additional video clips to follow the opening credits. Drag and drop the images from your collection and place them just behind the first image.

Using transitions with overlapping titles

So far you have learned how to insert titles into the opening credits. Titles can be used to give your viewers an outline of what is to follow in the next sequence. Titles are especially useful in initiating transitions to unrelated scenes or in explaining changes in content.

1 Run Paint. As an example, create four titles with a black background and text describing the various scenes. Some examples are shown below. Please also create an image with a black background and no text, in case you did not do so previously.

3. Titles that capture the imagination

2 Run Movie Maker.

3 Select *My Collections* on the left side of the window and right-click your mouse. Select *Import* in the subsequent menu. Use the *Select The File to Import* dialog box to locate the directory where your images are stored. In this particular example, six files are imported. To make multiple selections, click the first image; then press and hold (Ctrl) to select additional images. Once you have selected all required images, click *Open*.

4 Drag the first image from the *Collections* and place it in the first clip of the Storyboard.

5 Now drag the title into the second clip,

and insert the black image again, this time into the third segment.

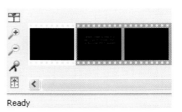

6 Insert the first video clip (for example arrival). Hold down the mouse and drag the clip from your *Collections* into the Storyboard.

7 Insert the black image just behind the clip.

8 Continue this process until you have inserted all clips and their corresponding titles.

9 Switch to the Timeline view by clicking the Timeline icon,

and decrease the playback duration of the still images to an acceptable limit, for example 3 seconds. For each clip, move the small triangle to the left until you have reached the desired mark. The triangles are used to specify the Mark-In/Out positions, and they are moved by clicking and holding down the mouse.

3. Titles that capture the imagination

The image on the monitor reflects the current position on the Timeline bar. As a final touch you can overlap images so that the subsequent image slowly comes into focus while the previous one fades out (soft transition).

Closing credits à la Hollywood

Towards the end of the movie, you have the opportunity to share additional information with your viewers. Use the *closing credits* to share important details with your audience:

- Who was involved in the creation of the movie?
- Who was responsible for what?
- When did you make the movie?
- What type of music did you use?

Credits: In the latter part of this chapter you learn how to use the closing credits to immortalize yourself as a director and cameraman.

Create all images for your closing credits using Paint, as you did with the opening credits (Chapter 3), and import the images into Movie Maker afterwards. Create the closing credits in the same way you created the opening credits. The various steps are not repeated here.

> *Note*
>
> **Animated text**
>
> Major commercial editing software packages feature powerful text editors, enabling you to create smooth transitions between various frames of text. In addition, you can use animation tools to slowly move the closing credits from the left side of your screen to the right. The only limit is your imagination. You can even create closing credits as seen on TV, where every person involved in the movie is listed alongside their screen names. These types of closing credits move from the bottom of your screen to the top.

Using still images from your video in the closing credits

By now you have learned how to create closing credits using the images created in the *Paint* graphics program. It is also possible to use a single clip from your video. Movie Maker has added functionality that allows you to create individual or still images using the Record tool.

45

4. Closing credits à la Hollywood

1 Connect your video camera to your PC using the Firewire cable and switch it on.

2 Start Movie Maker and select Record.

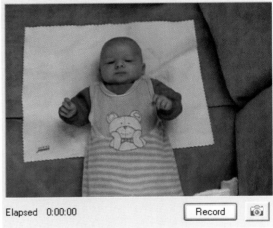

Notice a small camera icon to the right of Record.

Clicking this icon saves the current display as an image file. The file format is JPG, unlike Paint, which usually uses the BMP format.

JPEG Files

This type of file format has the ability to compress images to a high level with only a small deterioration in quality, requiring less disk space. Images seen on the Internet are usually stored as *JPG* or *JPEG* files. Another advantage to the JPEG file format is that you can select the level of compression.

Depending on the level of quality you want, you can compress your images to a high level. The higher the level of compression, the greater the deterioration in the quality of your images. Select the bandwidth for your type of Internet access and let the software do the rest.

Using still images from your video in the closing credits

3 Locate the image that you want to use in the closing credits and click the camera icon.

4 The Save window opens, prompting you to type a name for the image.

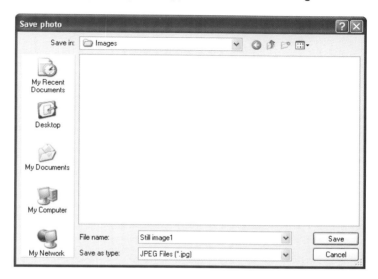

5 Save the image and close Movie Maker's Record tool.

6 Start *Paint* and open the new image you created.

4. Closing credits à la Hollywood

7 Select the Text tool and create a text box by dragging the crosshair cursor across the canvas.

8 Enter the closing text into the text box.

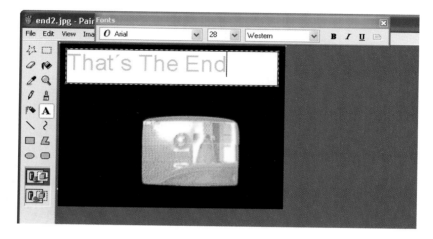

Do not forget to fill the white background of the text box with the overall background color.

9 Save the image as *24-Bit-Bitmap*.

Using still images from your video in the closing credits

The right type of image

If your video camera can be operated remotely, use Movie Maker's remote access capabilities. Select a section in your movie that does not contain a lot of movement. Fast panning shots can have a negative impact on your image and mightnot look good on screen.

10 Switch back to Movie Maker and go to *My Collections*.

11 Right-click your mouse and select *Import* in the subsequent pop-up menu to import the image that you just created.

12 Using the mouse, drag the closing image from *Collections* into the next available clip on the Storyboard.

13 Switch to the Timeline view by clicking the Timeline icon.

You can see the closing image appear at the end of your movie.

49

4. Closing credits à la Hollywood

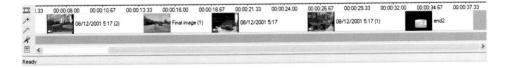

14 To invoke a soft transition from the last clip to the closing credits, select the closing image at the far end of the Timeline. Hold down the mouse button and drag the image to the left until it slightly overlaps the previous clip. The transition should take between two to three seconds.

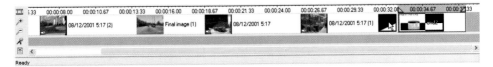

15 With the pointer inside the Timeline bar, right-click your mouse and select *Play Entire Storyboard/Timeline*. Move the slider in the preview window just ahead of the transition and press Play.

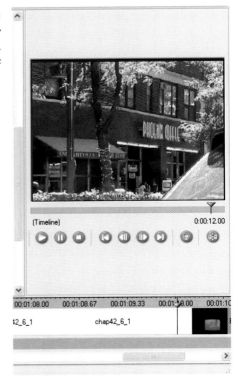

You discover what the transition looks like in your finished movie. Depending on the speed of your processor, it might be that the transition appears to be a little choppy.

Adding sound for greater impact

Imagine a Hollywood movie with no music and you realize why soundtracks replaced silent movies. The same is true for your digital video. It is more fun to watch a video when there is sound.

Note

Dramaturgy

Throughout a movie, sounds are strategically added to increase tension. Even with your own video production, audio components are almost always a necessary dramaturgical tool.

The video's own original soundtrack is rarely of good quality. Background noises can be disturbing as can be your own voice (or that of the video's maker giving instructions).

The problem is usually caused by the video camera's internal microphones. Often, these types of microphones are adequate for the immediate surroundings only. Outdoor recordings can be awful. Wind gusts, for example, can cause immense noise.

Film and video productions employ two types of audio categories: The original sound that is recorded at the same time as the video, and additional soundtracks, that are added later on. Adding sounds to the finished movie not only helps to set the mood. It is often necessary to add comments to allow your viewers to follow the story.

Adding comments later on

A good quality microphone is recommended for voice recordings. Cheap microphones specifically made for PCs are usually of the condensator type and produce poor quality recordings. Also, you can use high quality microphones when using your video camera outdoors.

Useful extras: The external microphone

If you own a video camera with an standard internal microphone, try using an additional one. Most video cameras can be connected to external microphones. Additional microphones are particularly necessary for outdoor recordings.

Microphone covers are also available to filter out disturbing background noise such as wind gusts. The range of available products includes everything from plain foam to heavy fur for use in particularly windy areas.

Dynamic microphones are recommended for voice recordings. Generally, frequencies between 50 and 12000 Hz should be sufficient; however, it would not hurt to add more. Dynamic microphones are particularly effective at close range and filter out background noise such as echoes in large rooms. Ensure that you can return the microphone to the vendor in case it does not meet your expectations.

Choosing the correct socket

Connect your microphone to the microphone socket of your sound card. Avoid using the *Line-In* or *AUX* sockets as the sound card drivers have been configured for best performance with the different types of sockets (that is, the different means of transferring sound). The various sockets are color coded. Refer to the sound card's manual for more information.

Prior to recording your comments, be sure to make some notes of what should be included in your narration. Take the time to watch your movie and determine the best segments to include your comments. Do a trial run by reading out your script while the movie is playing. This way you avoid embarrassing gaps and mistakes in the narration later on.

Adjusting audio settings

To ensure optimal sound recordings, you must adjust some of the sound card's default settings.

1 Go to *Start/Control Panel.*

3 Click the *Adjust the system volume* link.

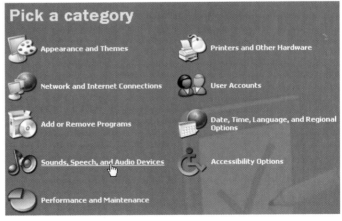

4 Select *Audio* in the next window.

Your PC's internal sound cards are listed under *Default Device*.

5 Select *Volume* in the *Sound recording* section.

5. Adding sound for greater impact

6 In the next window check the *Select* box below the *Microphone* section and drag the volume control to the halfway mark.

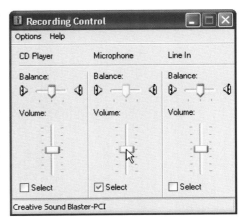

You can come back here to increase the volume further should you find that the volume is too low.

7 Close this window and click *OK* to close the remaining windows.

Recording voice files

There are two common approaches to recording voice files in Windows XP. You can use one of Windows' standard programs called *Sound Recorder* or use *Movie Maker*.

Additional audio tools

These days sound cards are shipped with a wide variety of additional software that is far more convenient to use than Windows' standard Sound Recorder program. Have a look at the available audio tools that were shipped with your sound card. Normally, video editing software packages also include their own tools for editing sound. The availability of these tools depends on the type of editing software you are using.

Using Movie Maker with digitally recorded sound

Because you are already familiar with Windows' Movie Maker, use it in this example to record your narration.

1 Start Movie Maker.

2 Switch to Timeline mode,

and click the microphone button in the bottom left corner.

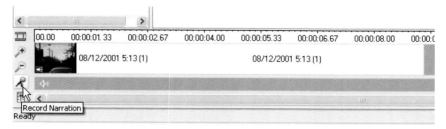

The *Record Narration Track* window opens up.

3 The *Line* setting has a default value of *CD-Audio*. Click *Change* and select *Microphone* in the *Input line* drop-down menu.

4 Click *OK* to return to the previous window. Click *Record to start recording through your microphone.* Read out your text but don't be too critical of yourself. It does not matter if gaps occur at the beginning and end of your narration. These can be cut later in Timeline mode. And if all else fails, you can always erase the recording.

5. Adding sound for greater impact

5 Click *Finish* after you have completed your narration. The *Save Narration Track Sound File* window opens up.

6 Give your file a meaningful name and save it on your hard drive.

Managing voice files

Using Windows Explorer, create a new folder called *Audio* in the *My Documents* direc-tory. Open the new folder and create a subfolder called *Narrations*.

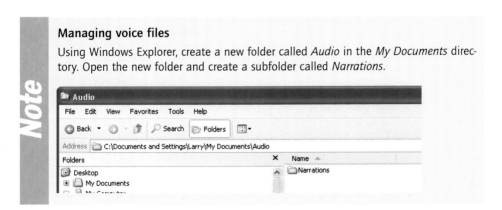

If the recording fails

The Record Narration Track window not only contains property settings but also has a multi-colored bar showing current volume levels. If the bar does not rise and fall during Record mode, no sound is being recorded. In this case please check the connections between your microphone and the sound card.

Once you have verified that all cables are properly in place, check the device manager to determine whether any problems occur relating to the sound card driver.

1 Go to *Start/Control Panel/Performance and Maintenance*.

5. Adding sound for greater impact

2 In the next window select *System*.

3 In *System Properties*, select the *Hardware* tab and click *Device Manager*.

The *Device Manager* opens up which contains information about your various hardware components.

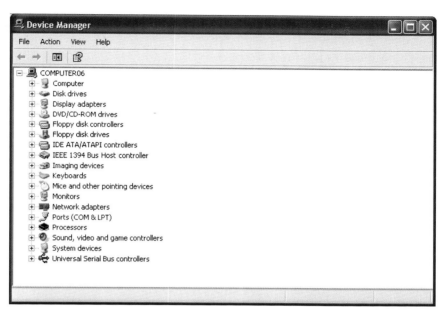

Unless you see a yellow exclamation mark within the Device Manager window, you should experience no problems with your device drivers. A yellow exclamation mark beside *Sound, video and games controllers* indicates that the audio driver is not functioning properly or not working at all. In this case you should reinstall the driver. If you have access to the Internet, go to the Web site of your sound card's manufacturer and download the latest driver available for your operating system.

Using the video camera to record sound

If you have an external microphone, you can create your own audio collection. Use your video camera to record sound. It is possible to create impressive sound effects using even the most basic tools.

5. Adding sound for greater impact

A fizzy drink, a squeaky door, running water, the twittering of birds, revving engines, a crying baby, and so forth.

Create sound files separately from your recording, just as you did with the voice files. Unlike the cables needed for recording through your microphone, use a cable for analog playback and connect it to your video camera. Usually, this type of cable has three plugs:

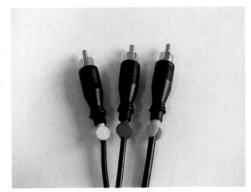

• one cable for video (yellow)

• and two for audio (white and red).

1 Connect the VHS cable to the analog socket of your video camera. Please refer to your camera's manual in case you are unsure about the location of these sockets.

2 You require an adapter to convert the video camera's two RCA plugs to a headphone type stereo connector.

3 Plug the connector into the *Line-In* socket of your sound card.

4 Run Microsoft Sound Recorder. Go to *Edit* and select *Audio Properties*.

5 Click *Volume* inside the *Sound re-cording* section.

6 Check the Select check box below *Line-In*.

This forces the Sound Recorder to use the Line-In socket of the sound card, rather than the microphone socket used in the previous example.

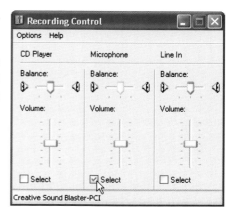

7 Close this window and click *OK* on all remaining windows. You can now record sound using your video camera.

Creating tension using background music

If you have suitable music on one of your CDs, start recording immediately.

Planning is important

Search your CD collection for suitable music. Watch your movie while listening to music that you think might work well with your video. Take your time because a good selection of music enhances the viewing experience of your audience.

If you do not have suitable music, ask your friends. Listen to a few songs and you soon have a feel for what works with your video generally or with certain sequences specifically.

Go reeeeeallly easy ;-)

Avoid using heavy beats as this may distract your viewers. Instrumental music is particularly effective, unless you are making a dance video.

Quite a few vendors of music are now specifically targeting video productions. The collection of available music covers everything from specific topics such as sports, travel, and so forth to individual sound bytes such as the twittering of birds, wind gusts, thunder, jet engines, squeaking doors, and engine sounds.

These pieces of music are usually licensed. Royalties are charged per second. The amount varies depending on the distribution of the movie. Private use is tolerated (the publishers really have no other choice as there are no controls in place to monitor private use).

License fees apply for public performances. If you intend to use your video commercially, you should contact your licensing agency. A large number of vendors offer unlicensed music for a one-time charge.

Copying a CD

1 Insert the CD into your CD-ROM or DVD drive. If the Media Player does not start automatically, go to *All Programs/Accessories/Entertainment/Windows Media Player*. Notice the CD's tracks listed on the left side.

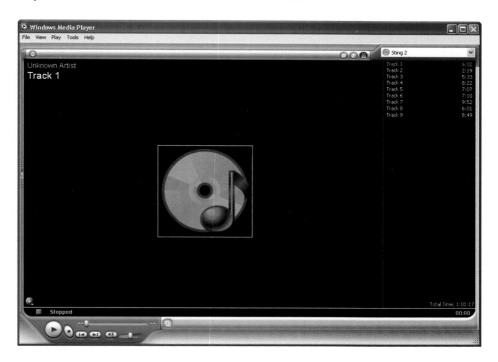

2 Select *File/Copy/Copy from Audio CD*. Select the tracks you want to copy to your hard drive. Click the individual songs. Next, click *Copy Music* (top right corner). *Copy Status* shows how far the process has progressed.

5. Adding sound for greater impact

Every time you want to use music from a CD, save the tracks to disk first.

Tracks are saved *under C:/My Documents/My Music*.

Full length tracks

The Media Player can only copy entire tracks. On occasion, a track might be too long for your video or a specific scene. You can work around this problem by editing the track in Movie Maker.

Inserting music into the video

To insert music into the video, follow these steps:

1 Run Movie Maker.

2 Insert a video clip into the Storyboard; then switch to Timeline mode.

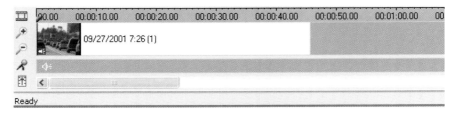

3 To switch to Timeline mode, click the *Timeline* icon.

4 Import one of the tracks you copied from CD. Right-click *Collections* and select the required track.

Music collections

It is a good idea to create a new collection called *Music* and save all tracks in this location. This archive can be easily accessed, but keep in mind that sound files can take up a lot of space on your hard drive.

Once you have imported the track, you can locate the file and its audio icon in your collection.

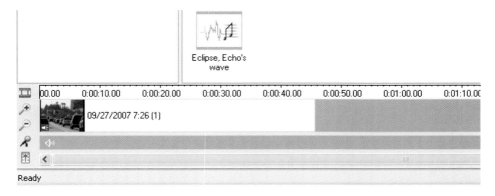

5. Adding sound for greater impact

5 Select the audio file. Click and drag the file into the audio bar next to the Microphone icon below the video.

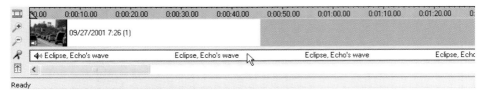

6 The audio clip used in the above example is too long for the video clip. Se-lect the audio clip and click Play in the monitor. The track plays. Click *Pause* once you have reached the portion of the song that you intend to use in your video. To eliminate the first 40 seconds in this example, insert a cut after the 40 seconds are up: Right-click your mouse on the audio clip; then select *Split* in the subsequent pop-up menu.

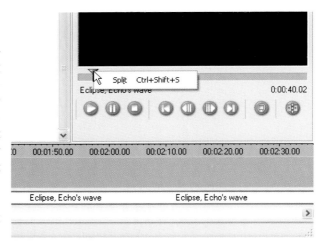

This action cuts the track into two separate audio files. The orginal file does not change.

7 Right-click the first audio clip and select *Delete* in the subsequent pop-up menu.
The audio clip is removed from the Timeline.

8 To synchronize the video and audio clips, click and drag the remaining audio
clip to the start of the Timeline.

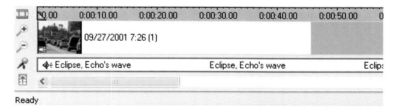

9 The audio clip is still too long and the end of the track needs to be cut.
Click the Zoom In icon twice to change the resolution of the Timeline.

10 Using the blue bar, move the Timeline over to the right until you reach the
end of the audio clip.

5. Adding sound for greater impact

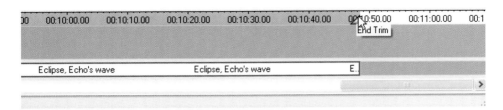

11 Press your mouse and drag the small triangle marking the end of the audio clip over to the end of the video clip. Make sure that the audio clip is active (active objects have a blue border).

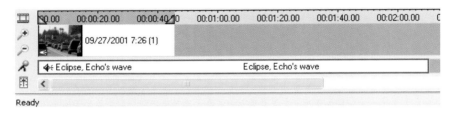

If the audio track is quite long, click the Zoom Out icon to decrease the resolution for the Timeline. This way you can see a greater portion of the file.

12 The soundtrack is not quite complete yet: By default, the pro- portion of the volume of added audio clips and the video's original soundtrack is 50/50. Click *Set audio levels*.

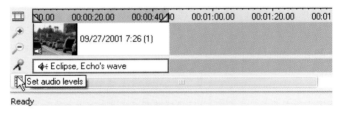

This opens the Audio Levels dialog box.

Move the slider to the right to increase the volume of the added soundtrack (moving it to the far right eliminates the original sound). Move the slider to the left to increase the vol-

ume of the video's original sound (moving the slider to the far left eliminates the added soundtrack).

70

13 If you only want to hear the music you added, move the marker all the way to the right and close the window.

The soundtrack is now complete.

Combining background music and commentary

It is possible to add background music to a video that has already had commentary added to it. Movie Maker only has one track for sound; therefore, you can only add one audio track at a time.

It is possible to work around this problem: Save the video after the background music was added and then reopen it in Movie Maker. Insert the remaining commentary and sounds on top of the background music.

1 After adding the audio tracks, save your video as a DV AVI file. In Movie Maker, select *File/Save Movie*.

5. Adding sound for greater impact

2 In the subsequent window, go to Setting: *Other*.

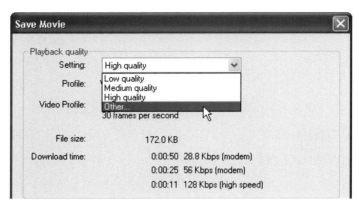

3 Under Profile, select DV-AVI NTSC (25 Mbit/s).

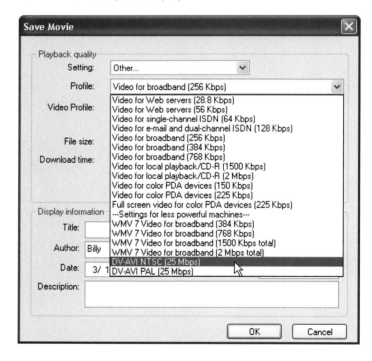

4 Click *OK* and then name the file and select *Save*.

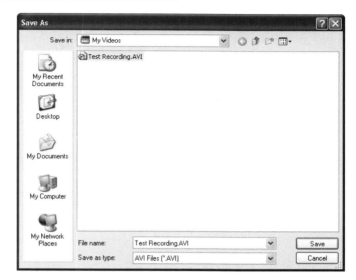

5 Your movie is created and the status of the export process is shown in the progress bar.

6 Open a new project in Movie Maker and import the clip you have just created into the Timeline. To do so, right-click *Collections* and select *Import* in the pop-up menu.

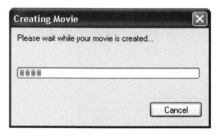

7 Drag the clip into the Storyboad; then switch into Timeline mode.

Correctly aligning audio files

Every time you insert an audio file you should preview your movie to ensure that it has been added at the appropriate moment. Right-click your mouse on the Timeline and select *Play Entire Storyboard/Timeline*. Click the Zoom In icon to increase the resolution of the Timeline. You can now place audio files with greater precision by moving them slightly to the left or right.

5. Adding sound for greater impact

8 Activate the collection that contains your sound and voice files.

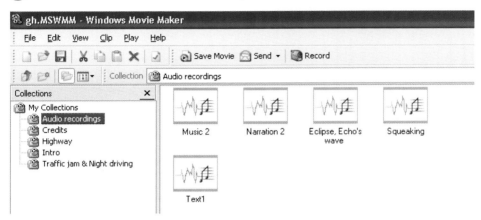

9 Click and drag the sound and voice files into the Timeline audio bar.

10 To adjust the respective volumes of background music and commentary, click the *Set audio levels* icon.

11 Depending on the respective volumes of commentary and background music, select these approximate settings:

Should your background music be too loud still and you cannot hear the commentary clearly, move the slider further to the right. Close the window and click Play in the preview pane.

Note

Save your project regularly

Save your project! You can always edit it later. To save it, go to *File/Save Project*. Make a habit of regularly saving your project by clicking the Save Project icon. It might never happen, but it is possible for Movie Maker to crash. It would be a shame if you lost several hours of work. You can also give your projects different names. For example, you could save the opening credits clips under *Opening Credits*. Next time you save your project, call it something like *First Scene*. This allows you to go back to individual segments later on and edit them if necessary.

Using overlapping sounds with different scenes

Similar to video clips, Movie Maker allows you to overlap audio clips.

1 Run Movie Maker and open the project you saved in the earlier chapter.

2 In the example, *Narration 2* is a voice file, and *Squeaking* is an audio file. To have the squeaking sound overlap with the narration, click and drag the file onto the narration segment.

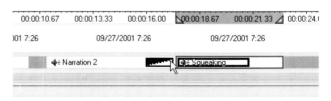

The black and white area shows the duration of the transition. *Squeaking* overlaps *Narration 2* by approximately one second.

75

5. Adding sound for greater impact

Release the mouse button. The overlapping sections of both files are identified by a dark grey hue.

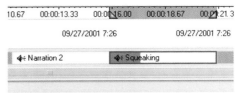

Sounds and music for your video

Fifty percent of a video is made up of sounds, commentary, and music. However, only a few of us can compose music and sounds on the computer. Various manufacturers have devised products to fill this obvious gap, although these types of products can be quite expensive.

That's why many vendors of video editing software packages are offering CD-ROMs with a huge variety of music and sound samples. These tracks are free for personal use.

Your local bookstore might stock a large variety of CDs with hundreds of different sounds. Prices are usually around $12.

The Internet – A sound archive

The Internet is full of sounds. However, free sound archives aren't always what they seem: The good ones are not usually free, and the free ones are not usually good. Furthermore, copyright issues are not always addressed.

Having said that, if you take your time searching the Internet, you might come across some good quality and even amusing or unusual sounds.

For example, use the Hotbot search engine (*http://hotbot.lycos.com*).

Enter your key words in *Search Smarter* (for example, car, laughter, or water). It is important that you check *MP3* in the *Page Must Include* section. If you fail to check this option, the search results include pages that merely contain text references to your key words but no audio files.

WAV and MP3

Sounds and music are usually available as *WAV* or *MP3* files. For our purposes, the file format is irrelevant. The advantage of MP3 is the higher level of compression. Music CDs have an approximate size of 700 MByte. The size of the same number of tracks saved as MP3 files would be approximately 1/10th of that, that is, around 70 Mbyte. This saves a large amount of disk space. Downloading music off the Internet only really became a viable option after the introduction of the MP3 format.

5. Adding sound for greater impact

Another excellent search engine is Google. As with Hotbot, enter your key words into the search text box.

Advanced search

Search for multiple key words and use the plus operator for the best results. Insert a space in front of the plus sign, for example: *free +sounds*. Also try: *squeaking +mp3*.

Making videos using Easy Video Producer

Throughout the first five chapters, Movie Maker was used to introduce you to the basics of video editing because most people who own a relatively new PC have access to this software.

Movie Maker allows you to perform quite a few tasks. You recorded your video and edited it, you inserted opening credits and added the soundtrack. However, you needed to use another program to create titles.

Although Movie Maker has quite a few good features, other commercial programs are available that cater to the requirements of entry level video editors and offer significantly more tools. One example is DATA BECKER's Easy Video Producer. Find out below how easy it is to:

- create animated opening credits
- insert overlapping transitions
- create subtitles
- overlay videos with picture-in-picture effects
- create time lapse and slow-motion effects
- add multiple soundtracks
- fade music in and out

Animated opening credits

When you run Easy Video Producer, the first window to open is the Start dialog screen. Select your project in this window.

79

6. Making videos using Easy Video Producer

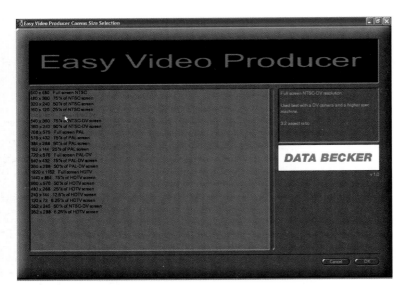

Because you are working in DV mode, select *720x480 Full screen NTSC-DV* from the menu and click *OK*.

This activates Easy Video Producer's main window, which is currently empty.

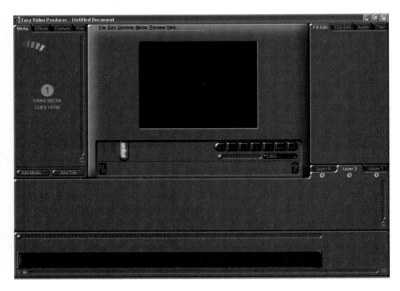

Look for the Media pane on the left. Import the video clips you want to edit into this area. Because you already used Movie Maker to record video clips in earlier projects, select *Add Media* and then select all video and audio clips that you want to use. These are automatically imported into the Media pane.

Optionally, drag the files from Windows Explorer and drop them into this window.

Click *Add Title* in the Media pane to add the opening credits.

The title is added to the Media pane with a default name of *My Title*.

To use this title, drag it onto the Storyboard and adjust its properties in the Title pane on the right. The pane contains the controls for color, font, and font size.

Change the default settings here. Click *Advanced* to change the advanced properties of your text.

You can choose to add shadows to your text. The arrows around the letter *A* on the icon in the bottom left corner determine the direction the shadow is cast. You can also adjust the transparency and color.

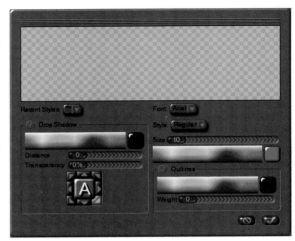

Go back to the Titler window to animate the opening credits. For example, to make the text curl around itself, switch to the effects pane, *FX Edit*.

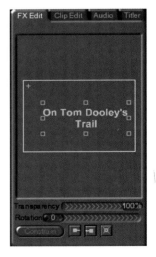

Click the yellow squares to expand or reduce the title. The buttons next to *Constrain* specify the Mark-In- and Mark-Out points, that is, the image after which the animation begins and where it ends. The purpose of the third button is to remove all animation in case something goes wrong.

Start by clicking the left button to specify the starting position or Mark-In point of the animation Then move the rotation slider until the title is almost entirely removed from the window.

Select the Mark-Out point to specify the end of the animation. Click the Mark-Out button and set the rotation slider to 0.

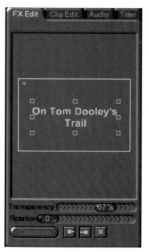

You might want to add another title to give additional information about the next clip. Go to Media and click *Add Title* and drag the title onto the Storyboard.

6. Making videos using Easy Video Producer

Use your mouse to select the title, go to the title editor, and enter your text. Remember that *shadows* can be added in the *Advanced* properties.

To do so, select the text in the title window and click *Advanced*. Check *Drop Shadow* and select a color from the color pallette. Choose a distance of approximately *4*, so that the main focus is not diverted from the title to its shadow.

Save your changes by clicking the green checkmark in the bottom right corner.

The software automatically creates a dissolve lasting two seconds.

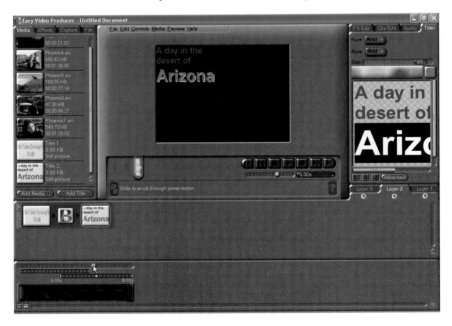

To decrease the duration of the transition to approximately one second, click the lower film strip, click and drag the strip slightly over to the right.

The opening credits are now done. This is a good time to save your project so that you do not have to start from scratch should the program crash. Saving the project allows you to edit this project at a later date. To save your project, select *File/Save presentation as...* from within the main window.

Enter the name and path of your project.

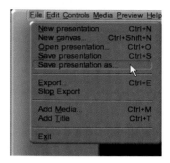

Versatile transitional effects

As with Movie Maker, soft transitions are applied by default when clips are added to the Storyboard.

Unlike Movie Maker, however, Easy Video Producer offers a large variety of transitions. Select one from the Effects tab and drag it onto the existing transition inside the Storyboard.

Click a transition type inside the Storyboard to further edit it in the Effects window on the right.

Different options are available, depending on the type of transition you are using.

Creating impressive transitions using overlaps

Easy Video Producer has three video tracks, allowing you to create impressive transitional effects combining titles, images, and videos.

For example, it is easy to add subtitles. Insert a new title by selecting *Add Title* in the Media palette; then switch to *FX-Edit* to change the position of the title.

Ensure that the title is located on the third track so that it is shown on top of the video. To achieve this, switch to layer three of the Storyboard and drag the title onto the Storyboard.

Switch to the *FX-Edit* window on the right to change the position of the title. This places the contents of layer two (the video) beneath the title.

Within FX-Edit, use your mouse to drag the text box to the desired location.

The yellow squares allow you to adjust the text. In this example, the text was justified to fit the full width of screen.

Picture in picture. It's possible!

Multiple video tracks enable you to create picture-in-picture effects. To use this functionality, ensure that your video files are located on two different layers. Ideally, place the second video one layer up from the main video. In our example, the video of the young man is located on layer three.

Within the FX-Edit window, adjust the size of the image and use your mouse to move it into the desired position. Switch back to layer two to view the results. Because the video on layer three is still active, you can make changes to the top image from here.

Slowing down, speeding up

With Easy Video Producer it is easy to create time lapse and slow-motion effects. If you want to increase or decrease the duration of a clip, its speed changes accordingly. Assuming that the original clip is 18 seconds long, and you shorten it to 9 seconds, the clip runs twice as fast. Its speed increases by 200%.

Drag the clip onto the Storyboard; then switch to the Clip-Edit window on the right. The double-sided arrow is used to increase or decrease the duration of the clip. Use this approach to change its speed.

Within the Timeline, click the right edge of the clip and drag it over to the left or right side until you have reached the desired speed. release the mouse button when you are done. These new settings are automatically stored. Check the speed at any time from within the Clip-Edit window.

6. Making videos using Easy Video Producer

Depending on the speed of your PC's processor, you might find that the result is not displayed in real time. Be patient. Even if the image you are viewing now is skewed, it will be properly displayed when viewed in full screen. The distortion is caused because the two halves of a panning shot are being displayed.

Adding Music to your video

The Easy Video Producer software allows you to easily add a soundtrack or commentary using its three audio layers.

If you want to add background music to your clip, drag the sound file onto the first track. Locate the volume settings on the right on the *Audio* tab. Use *Master* to adjust the overall volume. Next to Master you can see the volume control for the background music, which you placed on the first track. Move the slider down to decrease the volume of the selected audio file. In the example, the background music is quite low.

Drag the original video clip onto the second layer. The controls for the master volume and the video clip's original audio volume are located on the audio tab on the right of the window. In the example, the playback volume is increased slightly to compensate for the low volume of the video's original sound.

91

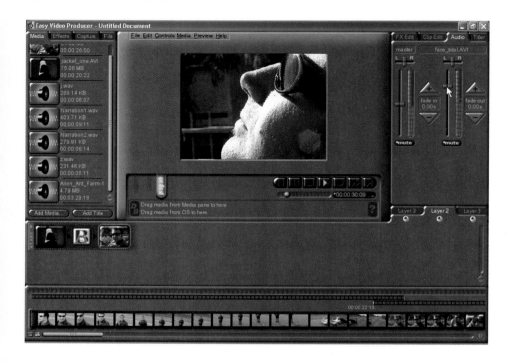

Adding a commentary to the clip

Once you have added the background music, you might want to add further comments explaining specific scenes. As a prerequisite, you should already have saved your narration to file and imported the file into Easy Video Producer's Media pane.

The first layer contains the background music discretely playing throughout the duration of the video. The second track contains the video with its original soundtrack. Therefore, the commentary must be placed *on top of* the first two layers. To do so, switch to the Storyboard and drag the audio file from the Media pane onto layer three.

Use the round blue button to position the clip at the appropriate section in the Storyboard. Switch to Clip Edit view and activate the shift mode by clicking the green film strip below the lock icon.

To increase the resolution of the Timeline, click the timescale increase button repeatedly. Locate this button in the bottom left corner of the Timeline.

To move the audio clip, click and hold in the center of the object and then drag it into the correct position.

6. Making videos using Easy Video Producer

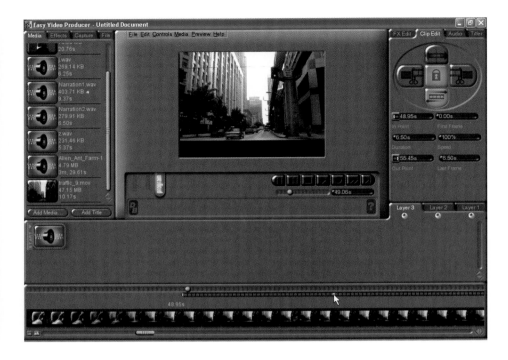

To distinguish the commentary from other background sounds, increase its volume in the Audio window.

Fading in sound

The volume controls of Easy Video Producer are user friendly. Notice two triangles next to the volume control.. Use the upper triangle to increase the duration of the transition by 0.2 seconds per mouse click. The duration of the transition is shown between the two triangles.

In the example, the duration of the transition is two seconds.

In case the duration of the transition is too long, decrease it by click-ing the lower triangle.

Saving & exporting video material

The last step of video editing is creating the final version of the finished cut video material. Most of the time, it is transferred onto the videotape of the camcorder again.

You can generally differentiate between creating a final version back on videotape (analog and digital) and saving the video in a hardware-independent format, which allows you to view the video on any PC or DVD player.

You should be able to play back PC videos without any special video hardware; however, the videos must be compressed in a certain way to ensure that they can also be played back on the PCs of your acquaintances and friends.

In addition, the type of compression used is especially important. You must be able to pass on your videos in the best possible quality without having to upgrade your hard disk just because the videos might be too big to send them by e-mail or because it might take hours to download them from the Internet.

Final check before creating the final version

Before you create the final version of your finished cut video, you must double-check the video to ensure it is sequenced correctly: Previewing critical parts of the video is important before the video is processed. These parts include the dissolves as well as the cut between two audio clips. A reprocessing of the entire movie because you overlooked a small mistake can be quite annoying because it can take quite long, depending on the size of the movie. Double-checking these parts of your movie can save you a lot of time and work.

Now take your time and go through the entire video again. You can also select critical parts of your video on the timeline and review only these again.

1 It's best to view the movie in full screen mode to ensure that you don't miss any details. To do so, right-click the timeline in Movie Maker and select the entry *Play Entire Storyboard/Timeline* from the pop-up menu.

2 Then click *Play* in the preview window;

3 and afterwards, click the full screen button.

Rendering the finished video

No matter which type you choose for the final version of your video, it always has to be *rendered*. This term is used to describe the calculating process of data such as the video effects, for instance. Rendering occurs only when the video is reprocessed after the actual video cutting. The effects added on the timeline are then applied to the original material and processed.

Thereby, special emphasis is placed on the type of processing whose final result is the new video clip. Your recorded clips remain unchanged on the hard disk of your computer.

The rendering process might take quite a long time, depending on the rendering settings you choose. The original video data is thereby considered source material. Any cross-fades, commentaries, background music as well as opening and closing credits are added on top of that. All this data is included in the rendering to create a new video

file. This is why the rendering process of videos takes such a long time.

Take into consideration that, as a result, your DV video clip must fit on your hard disk twice. To prevent any space problems, you should delete unused clips from your hard disk.

Smart rendering and background rendering

Some video editing programs offer the *smart rendering* function, which can be used to reprocess only the changes made to the video. This function not only saves time when creating the final version of your video but also ensures that the video quality of unmodified parts is maintained.

A few programs also offer *background rendering*. With this feature, the video is preprocessed in the background while you work on the timeline, that is, while you can define your cross-fades and credits. This way your system is used to its optimum, and the entire rendering of the movie doesn't take that long later on. If you still find mistakes after rendering the video, you can correct these quickly and then create the final version of your video.

Creating simple PC files

Movie Maker offers a number of presets. These can be used for exporting videos to customize the quality of your videos according to your own needs.

What's hidden behind WMV?

Apart from DV videos, Movie Maker always saves videos as *WMV* (Windows Media Video) files. However, another format is hidden behind WMV: ASF with the MPEG4 codec. ASF (Advanced Streaming Format) is capable of high compression. At the moment, ASF and WMV are not as popular as REAL (see below). Furthermore, ASF and WMV videos cannot be viewed if Linux is being used. WMV, however, is well suited to PC files because of the adjustable compression rate.

In the following, you create a PC file, which might not be commercial-class in terms of quality, but it is more than sufficient to send the video to your acquaintances and friends.

1 Once you have finished cutting your video and you've double-checked it, click *File/Save Movie*.

2 You can then see a selection of preset quality settings. Click

Other and confirm your selection with *OK*.

The first three entries are vague. They don't provide much insight into how the videos are configured.

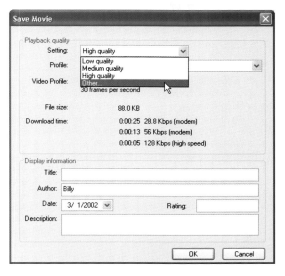

3 Under *Profile*, you can find a more extended and more detailed list of video profiles from which you can select different profiles. The best results occur if you choose DV-AVI NTSC. Always select this profile if you intend to edit the file further or if it is to be compressed in a different program, because at this setting hard-

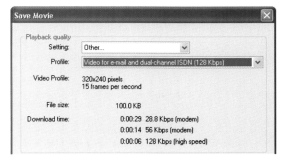

ly any quality loss occurs. Unfortunately, the file size is also relatively large.

For now, be content with a smaller file. Select the entry *Video for e-mail and dual-channel ISDN (128 Kbps)*, and confirm your selection with OK.

7. Saving & exporting video material

4 Enter the file name and save the destination of your video in the save dialog window that then opens. Once saving is complete, Movie Maker once again prompts you:

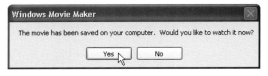

Watch the video after saving it. The result is already satisfactory. The file size of this example is 776KB. You can, however, detect a number of errors in the video. The audio part seems to be fine and is useable.

5 Now save your video again. This time, select the WMV 7 *Video for broadband (1500Kbps total)*. As you can see, the saved video is of good quality.

These examples have clearly illustrated that – depending on the application – it is important to select the proper export format.

Save space on your hard disk: DivX

For some time now, a new codec for AVI movies has been floating around called DivX. DivX allows you to save your movie in MPEG 4 format. In DivX-MPEG 4 format, it is possible to reduce the content of a DVD 10 to 12 times and still obtain better quality than a VHS recording. Instead of 6GB, for instance, a two-hour-long movie would be 700 MB in size. This way, you also have a suitable format at your disposal to save your DVD video digitally: these are just regular CD-ROMs, available for about US$ 0.50 a piece (Amazon.com).

Because Movie Maker cannot create DivX compressed videos, you must fall back on Easy Video Producer. Many other video editing programs are available, however, that work in a similar fashion.

7. Saving & exporting video material

DivX alias MPEG-4

Microsoft's first implementation of MPEG 4 is automatically installed with every Windows operating system since Windows 98. It is limited to a maximum data rate of 256 Kbps, which is far too small for a smoothly running video at a high resolution and of good quality. The DivX codec allows bit rates of 6000 Kbps. To cram a 120-minute-long movie onto a CD with 650 MB, a data rate of only 600 Kbps is already sufficient, however. With data rates of 1500 Kbps for 90 minutes spread over two CDs, the picture can hardly be distinguished from a DVD. DivX looks after the video material – MP3 is used most often for audio material. This is why the download bundle of DivX also contains an MP3 encoder. Please take into consideration that no DivX movies can be played back on your computer if you are only running the standard installation of Windows. You must first download the corresponding driver (codec) from the Internet and then install it. You can find this codec at *www.divx.com*. The bundle also contains a playback program. If you only install the codecs, Windows Media Player can also play back your DivX videos. "The Playa" is therefore not essential.

If you want to learn more about DivX, read the book *Fast Byte – DivX*, which has also been published by DATA BECKER. Check it out at *www.databecker.com*.

1 Start Easy Video Producer and select the desired video profile. In this example, *320x240* was selected. Confirm your selection by clicking *OK* at the bottom right.

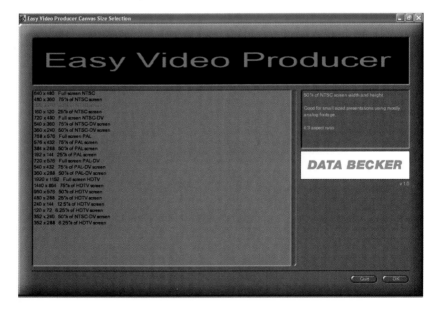

2 Import your video into the media archive of Easy Video Producer, for example, the video you created in Movie Maker that you might have rendered in DV NTSC. You can now process the video further. To do so, click *Add Media* and select your video from the file selection window that appears.

3 Drag the video from the media pane onto the storyboard.

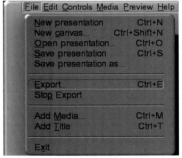

4 Because the video is not going to be edited further, you can select the *Export* entry from the *File* menu in the center window.

5 Select the export format *AVI Movie.* Under Video Codec, you must select the entry *DivX Codec* from the list.

The compression parameter, which is set at about 90%, should remain at about the same setting. If you decrease the parameter, the quality of the video is a little bit worse. The file size, however, is reduced drastically this way.

Click the green checkmark to start the export process.

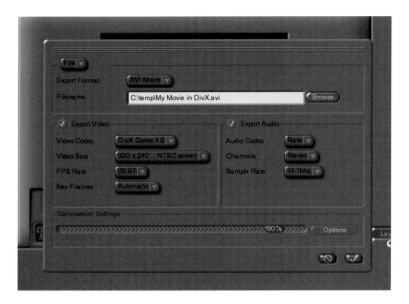

6 The small, blue bar indicates the export status. Once the export has finished (you are not notified once the bar has moved all the way to the right), you can play the video back in Media Player.

Creating video CDs

MPEG formats are the worldwide standard for digital video – from DVD to digital TV. A highly sophisticated technique is behind this format that can compress videos by a thousand fold – without any visible loss in quality.

What's behind MPEG?

In the USA and Japan, NTSC is the common format, using a resolution of 720x480 pixels at a color depth of 24 bit and 30 images. The signals are thereby not available within the RGB color range, which is the normal range for computer monitors. Instead, they are converted to Y (luminance information), Cb (blue-yellow balance) and Cr (red-green balance). Because the human eye is poorer at perceiving color nuances than it is at detecting differences in luminosity, the two color components can be reduced by half without any significant loss in quality.

In NTSC, such a video signal would still create a data quantity of approximately 30 MB/s of studio quality material. Because the average PC or other devices used in entertainment electronics can hardly process such signals, the data rate has to be drastically reduced at the expense of quality. All of the well-known manufacturers and users of such technology have agreed to use MPEG-2 as the data compression method in digital TV and for the playback of DVDs. This way, digital TV programs with data rates of 4 to 6 Mbps can be broadcast and only require 30 to 45 MB of hard disk space per minute.

MPEG-2 allows for *variable* or *adaptive* data rates – the amount of data is not constant when processed but is adjusted to the actual requirement of the picture's contents.

The MPEG-2 standard has been in effect since 1995, providing studio quality for digital TV in the range of 8Mbit/s, and can also be used for high definition TV (HDTV). All of the worldwide projects to introduce new digital TV transmission norms rely on MPEG-2, despite all incompatibilities such as frequencies and resolution.

Note

Creating a Video-CD file with TMPEG

The program *TMPGEnc* enables you to create MPEG-1 and MPEG-2 files from AVI files that were produced in Movie Maker (or any other program). You can find and download TMPGEnc at the following Web site: *www.tmpgenc.com*.

The creation of *video CDs* and *Super Video CDs* is particularly interesting. If you are interested in this subject matter and you want to delve into it, pick up a copy of *Fast Bytes – Create Video CD's*, which has also been published by DATA BECKER.

7. Saving & exporting video material

Video CDs

An MPEG-1 video usually has 352x240 pixels in NTSC; this means that the video image is only a quarter of the original size. One disadvantage of MPEG-1 is the constant speed when processing the data: Whereas critical scenes containing lots of movement require more data to ensure a satisfactory image quality, static scenes require less data.

However, video CDs can be played back on your PC as well as on most DVD players. Compared to the ancient VHS tape, CDs are not only considerably less expensive but also a lot more durable.

1 Start TMPGEnc. At the bottom right, select the option *System (Video+Audio)* from the *Stream type* section.

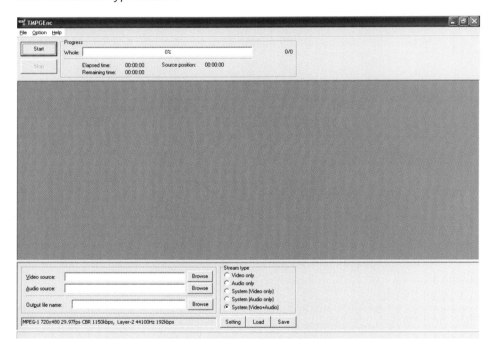

2 Click *Load* afterwards and select the *VideoCD (NTSC).mcf* profile. You have now loaded the required profile to ensure that the video CD complies with the standard and can, for instance, be played back with a DVD player.

3 You are then brought back to the main window. Now, you only have to specify the source files. TMPGEnc distinguishes between source files for video and audio. Because you have already cut your video and finalized the audio for it, you must select the same files for video and audio.

Under *Video source*, click *Browse*. Select your video file from the dialog window and confirm your selection with *OK*. In case the same file is not automatically entered under *Audio source*, you must click *Browse* again; then select the same file you chose under *Video source*.

4 Under *Output file name*, enter the file name for the export file. To do so, click *Browse* again and select the file path.

5 All settings required to create your video CD have now been defined. Click *Start* in the main program window.

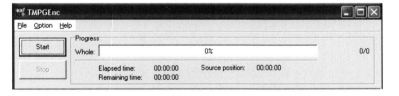

A progress bar is displayed that informs you about the status of the export process.

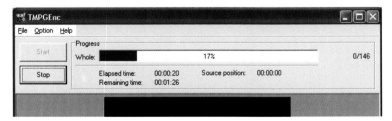

Depending on the length of your video and the system processor used, the export might take a number of hours. It takes even longer to create Super Video CDs because of the high compression of the video data, which requires extensive and time-consuming calculations.

You can now watch the created MPEG file with Windows Media Player by double-clicking it in Explorer. You do not need to install any additional software.

Burning a video CD with NERO

The MPEG-1 video files created in TMPGEnc can be immortalized on a simple CD-ROM, the *video CD,* by using burn software. The video CD has its origins in Asia, where you can still find video stores offering a large selection of this type of media instead of the VHS tapes, which are more familiar to us.

Video CDs can be played back on most DVD players. For many video-editing amateurs, this is even a reason for purchasing one because it is possible to store a relatively large amount of video material on these small discs.

The "real" DVD player

If you want to purchase a DVD player, you should make sure that it is able to play back video CDs and Super Video CDs apart from regular DVDs. This way you use the best technology currently available and won't need to fall back on outdated technologies such as the VHS standard to show your videos.

Burning a video CD is really simple.

1 Start your burning software. (This example uses *Nero*.) Select *Compile a new CD*, and click *Next*.

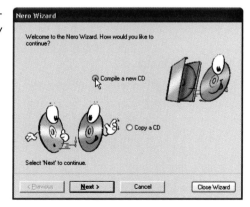

2 In the next dialog window, select *Other CD formats* and click *Next*.

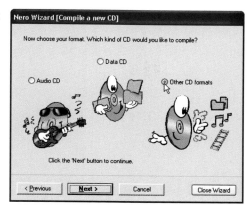

3 Under *Other CD formats*, select *Video CD*.

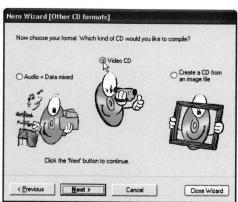

4 The wizard provides you with some information in the last window: If you are using AVI instead of MPG/MPEG files, Nero automatically converts the files. The quality of these files, however, is not as good as the quality of files created in TMPGEnc. Click *Finish* to proceed.

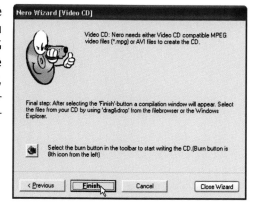

7. Saving & exporting video material

5 You are now in the main program window of Nero. Use the file browser on the right to locate the files to be burned on your Video CD. It is also possible to drag a number of files one after the other from the browser into the track window at the bottom left.

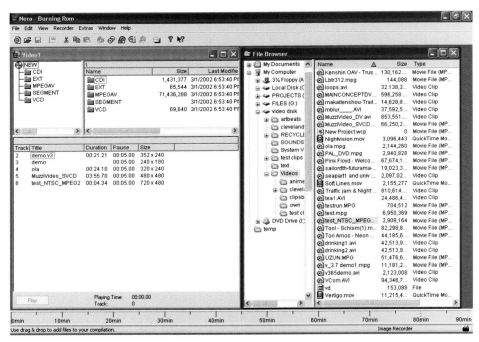

6 Once you have imported the desired file(s), select the entry *Write CD* from the *File* menu.

7 In this example, only the entry *Burn* can be selected in the *Burn CD* window. A test is not required anymore (therefore, the test option is not available), because the files were already checked during their importing.

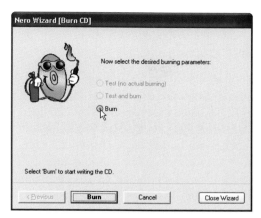

8 The dialog window displays the progress of the burning process. During the burning process, if possible you should not work on your PC because doing so might cause interruptions and lead to write errors on your CD. Use this opportunity for a coffee break!

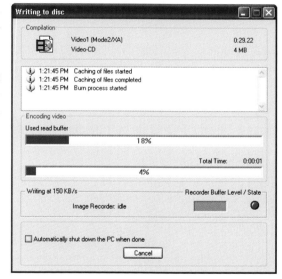

9 The procedure is now completed – you have done it!

You can now play back the CD on your PC or conveniently watch it on TV by using your DVD player.

Working like a pro: Super Video CD or MPEG-2

Digital videos eat up your hard disk space! One minute of digital video (AVI-DV NTSC) equals approximately 220 MB. For this reason, only about 3 minutes of video material fits on a regular CD. This format is therefore not suitable, and DV tapes are still too expensive to use them for archiving.

To store videos and ensure their good quality is maintained, choose a high-quality format that does not require a lot of space. Apart from the already mentioned DivX format or the video CD, the MPEG-2 format is well suited to this purpose and also popular among professionals. With *MPEG-2*, you can set different bit rates (that is, bits per second). This way you can decide for yourself which quality is best suited to your needs.

Digital TV and DVDs that can be purchased on the market are in MPEG-2 format.

Where's the trap?

The file size limitation of the AVI file format is – independent of the file system – 2 GB. This limitation affects all *Video for Windows codecs*. The newer AVI DirectShow filters can save videos as larger files. In Windows 98 and Windows ME, however, they are also limited to 4 GB because of the file system limitation. Only Windows 2000 and Windows XP support the writing of files larger than 4 GB, providing the NTFS file system is used. This does not apply to the old Video for Windows codecs, however. MPEG in itself does not have any limitations.

While watching the video CD, you certainly notice that some parts of the video display a couple of quality flaws, although the overall quality is perfectly satisfactory. The image might turn out to be scrambled, especially if a scene contains a lot of movement or a lot of details. You have another option to avoid this quality prob-

lem: Save your video in S-VCD format. In comparison to VCD, a different video resolution is used. In addition, MPEG-2 is the file format instead of MPEG1. Please take
into consideration, however, that a software DVD player has to be installed to play
back these video files. Quite a number of different players are available on the
market right now that, to some extent, can be acquired at no charge. A few DVD
players are also available that can play back the SVCD format.

Creating a Super Video CD

Under *Load*, select the SuperVideoCD profile in TMPGEnc. All you need to do now is
to set the desired bit rate under *Rate Control*. Make sure that if you add up the video
and audio bit rates, the total does not surpass 2600. You can find out more about
Super Video CDs in the book "Video: From VHS to DVD", which was also published
by DATA BECKER.

Simple MPEG-2 output

If it does not matter to you whether your MPEG-2 video can be played back with a
DVD player, you are, of course, free to choose another resolution under *Size* in
TMPEGEnc. (for example, full NTSC resolution at 720x480). To obtain better quality
or smaller files, you can also try a different data rate under *Rate Control Mode*. Give
it a try!

Transferring the final version back to your camcorder

Certainly the most elegant way is to transfer the finalized video back to your camcorder. This gives you the flexibility to play back your video anywhere at any time. To
watch your video on a TV, you need a conventional VCR or DVD player that has an
analog Video In. You can then transmit your video from the analog output of your
camcorder through your VCR to your TV.

7. Saving & exporting video material

To output your video through your camcorder again, three prerequisites must be met.

1. Your video has to be in DV-AVI format, whereby you must ensure that you comply with the corresponding video standards (NTSC in North America).

2. Your camcorder has to have a DV-IN.

3. The video editing software has to offer you a particular function with which you can output the saved DV video through your FireWire card.

To save your video as DV-AVI so you can play it back from your DV camcorder, proceed as follows in Movie Maker:

1 Once you have finished editing your project, select the entry *Save Movie* from the File menu.

2 Under *Setting* in the next dialog window, select *Other* and then *DV-AVI NTSC (25 Mbps)* from the available settings.

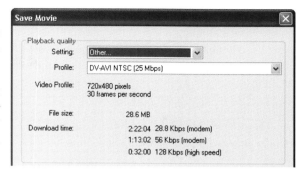

You can ignore the comments under *Download time* because the video is neither located on a Web server nor intended to be sent by e-mail.

Once the save procedure has finished, the video is in DV-AVI format and can be transferred to your camcorder again by using your FireWire card.

Because Movie Maker does not offer a function to directly transfer the file to your camcorder, you must use different software.

You could, for instance, download *MainActor* from www.mainconcept.com. This is a program bundle containing different modules. The module *DV-Out* is free of charge and can be used without limitation.

1 Start DV-Out from the Programs menu.

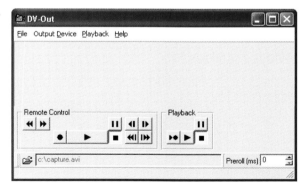

2 You can load your video file by clicking the file icon. DV-Out allows you to define the preroll of your camcorder.

The *Preroll* window displays the time period in milliseconds, which should elapse before your camcorder starts the capture once the video transmission is started. With this function, you can prevent the possible loss of the first few images of the video. The preroll time of your camcorder is provided in the camcorder manual. Most of Panasonic's devices, for instance, require 250 milliseconds of preroll time, which corresponds to a quarter of a second. Preroll 250 ms

3 Click the *Play/record* button to automatically start the video transmission to your camcorder. At the same time, your camera switches to recording mode.

Once the video has been transmitted, *Play/record* no longer appears depressed and the camcorder has stopped.

Transferring to a VCR

If your camcorder does not have a DV-IN, you still have the option of outputting your video through a graphics card to directly transfer it from your PC to your VCR, for instance.

Usually these cards have two outputs – an RCA output and a S-VHS output.

Output through the graphics card

1 Start the control center of your graphics card by clicking the screen settings button in the system tray.

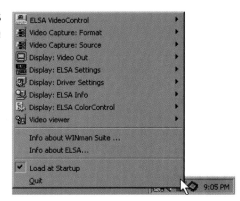

2 From the *Video Out* menu, select the video output configuration.

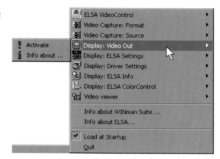

3 Enable the video output in the *Display* configuration window. There you can define which area you want to transfer through the video out. Here you can select *Video, Direct3D*. Please note that – depending on the graphics card you are using – the dialog windows might appear different. If you are unsure about how to activate the video from your graphics card, take a look in the manual of your graphics card or call the support-line of the manufacturer. You can usually get to this menu by right-clicking the desktop and selecting the option *Properties/ Settings/Advanced*.

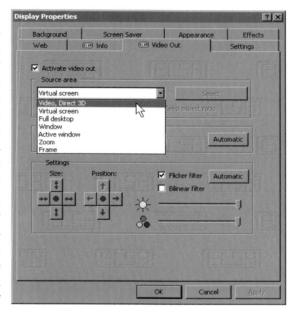

After confirming your settings with *OK*, the video signal transmitted by Media Player is redirected to the video out of your graphics card. You can then transfer the signal directly to your TV or loop it through the VCR. The advantage is that you can record the video directly.

Don't forget that you must tap into the sound through the line out of your sound card, as only the video part can be transmitted through the graphics card.

117

Which cables are important?

In the case of VHS, video as well as audio data is transferred. Very often, the different connectors used are confusing. Therefore, they have been assigned different colors:

Yellow for video, red for audio – right channel, white for audio – left channel.

In the case of S-VHS, the output is different: Only video information is transmitted through the S-VHS cable. This way, the data transfer is increased and a better video image is obtained. You must use an audio cable to transfer the audio data.

Sending videos through e-mail

You can e-mail videos directly from Movie Maker over the Internet.

1 Once you have edited your video, click *File/Send Movie To/E-mail*.

2 A dialog box opens so you can configure the export profile. Under *Setting*, you can define the quality of your video. The time required to download the video from the Internet is given under *Download time*. For this very short video, a download time of approximately 11 seconds

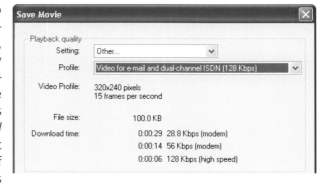

should be estimated if a 56 Kbps modem is used. Select the quality of the video under *Setting* and confirm your selection with *OK*.

3 A dialog window opens in which you must enter a file name for your video. Type the name into the text entry field and click *OK*.

119

7. Saving & exporting video material

4 The video is generated afterwards.

5 Once the video has been generated, a new dialog window opens. Here, you must specify the e-mail program you are using. Select the appropriate one from the list and confirm your selection with *OK*.

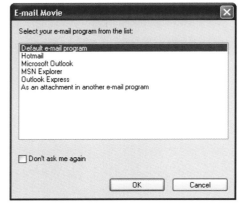

6 To send it, follow the subsequent instructions given by the program.

Digital images in a different way: The slide show!

Movie Maker does not only enable you to cut videos; you can also use its tools to create interesting slide shows. Because Movie Maker supports BMP and JPG files, any digital camera can be used.

How are the photos transferred?

Apart from digital cameras, you can also use camcorders to shoot still images. The images are usually saved on additional cards. These are connected to the USB interface – usually via an accessory device; the provided software undertakes the transfer of data and saves the images in the desired format on your hard disk.

Transferring photos from your camcorder to your PC

Some camcorders don't use any special memory cards. This is especially the case with first generation DV camcorders. These devices save the actual image for about 8 seconds as a still image when the trigger button is pressed. In this case, the corresponding camcorder sequence has to be recorded with Movie Maker.

1 Turn on your camcorder and use the FireWire cable to connect it to your PC.

2 Start Movie Maker.

3 Open the Record dialog window by clicking on the Record button. [Record]

4 Select *Other...* from the Setting options. In the pop-up menu that follows, you should select DV-AVI (25 Mbps) to obtain the best possible quality. Then use the camera controls to jump to the specific location of your images on the tape.

8. Digital images in a different way: The slide show!

Click the Pause button next.

Click on the button displaying the camera; a snapshot will be taken at the particular position of the tape you just stopped at.

5 A dialog window opens in which you can define a file name for your image. Movie Maker will then save the image in JPG format.

6 Proceed the same way until you have saved all of the images to be used for your slide show on the hard disk.

Transferring photos from a digital camera

It is pretty simple to transfer images from a digital camera. Surely, your digital camera came with a USB cable and a CD-ROM for the corresponding drivers. Of course the driver will have to be installed before the images can be transferred. During the installation of the driver, image editing software is usually automatically installed as well. You don't have to rely on this software, however, as any graphics software is able to import images from digital cameras by now. Only the driver has to be installed.

122

How are the photos transferred?

1 Turn on your camera and connect it to your PC (usually by using a USB cable).

2 Start your image editing program.

3 From the File menu, select the entry Import. In this case, this is the *Digital Camera Manager*.

4 The driver window of your camera will open afterwards. Please note that the window will appear different depending on the camera used. Select the menu entry Import images from this window. Very often, the term Import will be used in the menu.

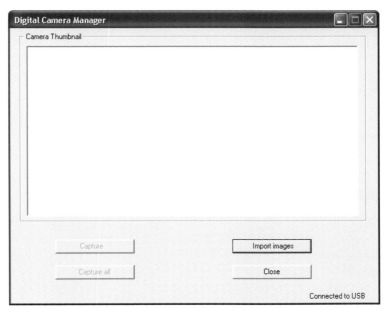

5 The image transfer might take a couple of minutes. Once it is finished, the images on the memory card of your camera will be listed.

6 In order to transfer all images to your hard disk, simply choose Capture all. You can also transfer specific images by selecting them with your mouse and pressing the Crtl key. Select Capture afterwards. Only the images you selected will be transferred to your hard disk.

7 Save the images. Don't change the resolution (or the image size) as the image quality would be decreased as a result.

Arranging images in Movie Maker

Once all of the images are located on your hard disk, you can start creating the slide show. In order to prepare the viewer and let them know what to expect, you should create appealing opening credits for the beginning of the show as you did with the video.

Creating the opening credits for your slide show

1 Start Microsoft Paint.

2 Select the entry *Open* from the File menu. Select one of the images you transferred from your camera onto the hard disk in the dialog window that follows. If possible, select meaningful image which will spark the viewer's curiosity.

3 The toolbar on the left contains the Rectangle tool. If you click on it, a palette will open further below containing 3 additional tools. Select the second tool which will create a framed rectangle displaying a white background.

4 Draw a rectangle; this rectangle will contain your introductory text for the slide show which will be created in the next steps. Now fill this area with a color which can be selected from the color palette at the bottom of the program window. Use the paint bucket tool to fill the area with color.

8. Digital images in a different way: The slide show!

5 Select the Text tool from the toolbar now, and draw a text window by using the cross-hair symbol which appears. Enter the title for your slide show in this window.

6 Fill the white background area with the same color again by using the paint bucket to put more emphasis on the text.

7 Save the image in BMP format.

Cross-fades during the slide show

Abrupt changes between images can appear disturbing to the viewer. At least when changing the subject matter, you should give the viewer the opportunity to prepare himself for the next sequence. You will certainly know this from slide shows: There are no sudden transitions between images; instead, one image fades off before the next one fades on.

Keep a black image ready for this purpose – use it the way you did in chapter 4.

Slide show with music and photographer's commentary

When transferring the images from your camera, you will certainly get an idea on how to arrange the images in your slide show.

8. Digital images in a different way: The slide show!

How about entertaining your viewers by providing additional information and pleasant background music? This has the advantage that you can e-mail your slide show or burn it on CD-ROM, and your friends and family will still be able to enjoy your commentary – even though they might be thousands of miles away.

For this purpose, you should write down notes about any picture which might require an explanation and record this information the way it was explained in chapter 5 by using a microphone. Because your commentary will be in digital format on your hard disk, you will be able to adjust the display time of the images to the length of your commentaries when cutting the slide show.

Pleasant music (maybe typical music from your vacation country) will give your slide show that additional holiday flair ...

Sequence of images

Have you finished all the preparations for your slide show? Have the images from your camera been transferred to your hard disk, the opening credits finished, the background music selected and the commentary already recorded? Then let's get started:

1 Start Movie Maker which will open in storyboard mode. This mode is perfect to arrange the images.

2 Switch to *View/Options* and enter how long the images should be displayed. In order to facilitate working with the timeline later on, you should not choose too short a time period. It will be easier to decrease the display time in the timeline view later on than to increase it.

3 Import all of the images you want to use into your collection.

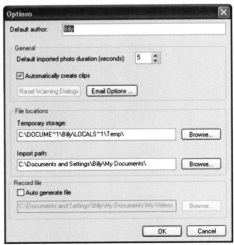

4 Drag the black image into the first box of the storyboard by keeping your mouse button depressed.

5 The opening credits will be inserted in the second box of the film strip. Next, the black image should be inserted again. This will increase the suspense ...

6 In sequence, drag all images which belong together into the storyboard. It's a good idea to insert the black image in between images of sandy beaches or sunsets, for instance, as this will create a dreamy mood.

8. Digital images in a different way: The slide show!

As a brief break for the viewers, you should always insert a black image after one group of images has been completed.

7 Continue the same way to insert the rest of your images into the storyboard.

8 In order to set the display time of the images, you will have to switch to timeline view now.

Click on the magnifier icon with the plus symbol on the left-hand side to increase the timeline's resolution.

Click on this button two to three times. As you can see, the resolution changes and you obtain a better overview of your project.

9 Select the first image and drag the small gray triangle located on top of the image to the right until a time period of 10 seconds is displayed in the preview window; then let go of the mouse button again. The display time has now been extended to 10 seconds. You have to select the image that follows the one where you just adjusted the time, and drag it to the right – then all of the images following that one will move automatically.

10 You can now drag your second image (with your title) over the first one so they overlap for about two seconds, for instance.

11 Decrease the display time of the adjacent black image to 3 seconds, for example. Then drag it over the image containing the opening credits and create an overlap of about one second.

12 Now it's up to you to decide on the style of your slide show:

Should the images be displayed immediately one after the other i.e. without any transitions in-between them? If you choose this option, you will only need to adjust the display time of the individual images to the commentary, for instance.

Or should the images softly fade into each other during the slide show? For this to occur, click on the corresponding image and adjust the display time by moving the small triangles of the individual segment Drag the adjacent image over the previous one in order to create an overlap of about one second.

Don't forget to save your project so that you can continue working on it later on.

Slide show with music

As with videos, you can make a slide show more interesting by adding background music.

1 Import the music files to be used into your collection. It's best to create a new collection e.g. Music Slide Show. It is easier to manage the titles this way. Your slide show will be even

more interesting if you use a separate piece of music for each section.

8. Digital images in a different way: The slide show!

2 From the new collection Music Slide Show, drag the audio clip for the opening credits into the audio bar of the timeline.

> **Is your audio clip too long?**
>
> Your audio clip will certainly be either too long or too short. Normally, the audio clip cannot be extended. Therefore, you will have to shorten or lengthen the opening credits. Simply modify the first and third image so that the opening credits are the same length as the audio clip.

3 Drag the remaining pieces of music to the corresponding audio bar position in the timeline, and adjust the display length of the images accordingly.

That's it! You have now added a soundtrack to your slide show. Again, save your project under a meaningful name. Then select the entry Save Movie from the File menu. In the dialog window that follows, select the option Other from the Setting pull-down menu. Under Profile, select the option DV-AVI NTSC and save your slide show.

Guiding through the show with commentaries

At the beginning of this chapter we mentioned briefly that adding commentaries to your slide show offers you a number of advantages. As with a live presentation, the viewers will obtain additional information about the individual images – of course only where additional comments are required. Another advantage is that you can take as much time as you need to prepare the slide show on your PC and think about the commentary for every interesting image. Once you have recorded your commentary on your PC using a microphone (see chapter 4), you can enhance your slide show with your own spoken commentary in addition to your music soundtrack.

1 Start Movie Maker again and import the slide show which you have just created into your collection.

2 Also import your commentaries which you have previously recorded into a new collection which you could call *Commentary Slide Show*, for instance.

3 Then drag the clip into the timeline.

4 As only the first image is displayed on the timeline now, you will have to use the preview window to precisely place your commentaries.

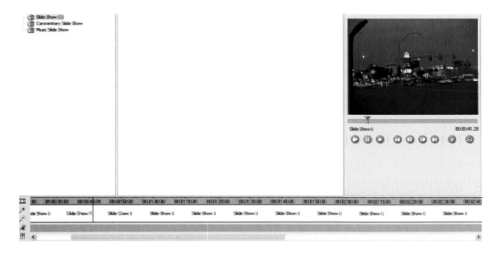

8. Digital images in a different way: The slide show!

Hereby, the sliders as well as the position display located underneath the preview window play an important role. Drag the slider to the right until the desired position appears in the preview window.

The timeline slider moves at the same time. Consequently, the exact position is also displayed on the timeline. Once you reach the position at which the commentary should be inserted, drag the commentary clip from the collection into the audio bar of the timeline.

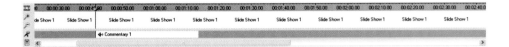

5 Proceed the same way until all of the commentaries are places at the correct timeline position.

6 As the last step, you might have to increase the volume level of your commentaries to keep the background music from being to prominent. This way you will prevent the spoken words from getting drowned out by the music soundtrack.

Click on the following button to open the audio level controls. In the dialog window that follows, move the slider to approximately the same position as illustrated here:

By changing the volume, the commentaries should be clearly audible, and the background music should – as the name suggests – only be in the background. Should the commentaries still not be loud enough, you can move the slider further to the right. If the background music is too quiet, you will have to move the slider somewhat to the left.

7 Once you have closed the audio levels window, you can save your project. Then select the entry Save Movie from the File menu; under Setting select the option *Other...* and under Profile, select Video for broadband *(1500 Kbps total) this time.*

The reason for saving it under a different profile is that you are working with indi-vidual images in a slide show; therefore, a quality at 1500 Kbps is sufficient. In addition, your slide show will not be too big this way so that you are able to create very extensive projects with it. One CD-ROM will this way provide enough space for a slide show of about 45 minutes in length.

Preparing your system for video editing

Video editing can quickly push your PC to its performance limits. A well-configured system is also a prerequisite for cutting videos on the computer.

To avoid dropouts (missing parts of the recorded video) during digitization, you must ensure that the hard disk and internal data transfer work as fast as possible. A number of system settings should always be optimized.

Preparing your hard disk

Prepare your hard disk before you start cutting your video to make sure everything runs smoothly.

Deleting unnecessary files

Delete all files on your hard disk that you don't need anymore, and don't forget to empty your recycle bin afterwards (you need a lot of space!):

On your desktop, right-click the recycle bin icon,

and select the entry *Empty Recycle Bin* from the pop-up menu. Confirm the next message box with *Yes*.

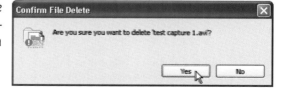

This process might take a little while.

Defragmentation

Due to regular operations, the hard disk space of your computer is fragmented. This means that your files are not always saved as one piece on the hard disk. Instead, they are scattered in small parts all over the hard disk, which greatly reduces the reading and writing speed of hard disks.

You can start the defragmentation program now: *Start/Programs/Accessories/System Tools/Disk Defragmenter*.

Once the *Disk Defragmenter* program has been started, select the hard disks to be defragmented from the list.

Select the hard disk and then click *Defragment*. The program might stop, and you might receive an error message such as *Disk Defragmenter cannot continue because an error has occurred*. In this case, you might have other programs running in the background that are accessing the hard disk. Close all programs and try it again.

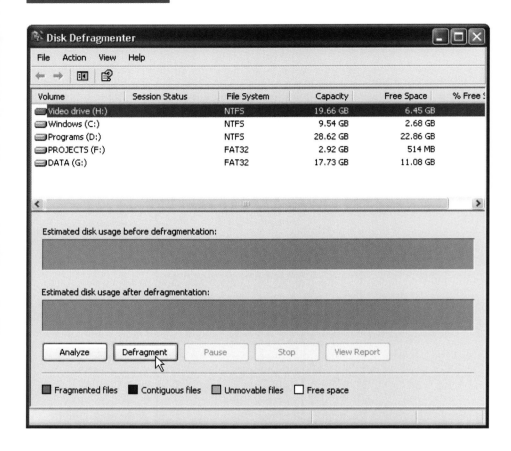

Faster drives: DMA

You might have already realized that hard disks and other data carriers are the bottlenecks in PCs. For this reason, access to them has to occur as fast as possible. At the same time, the processor should not be heavily burdened.

Today's PCs offer the DMA mode – Direct Memory Access – for this purpose, which allows you to bypass the processor, so to speak. To check whether DMA is enabled on your computer, open the *Start* menu and click *My Computer* and *Properties*.

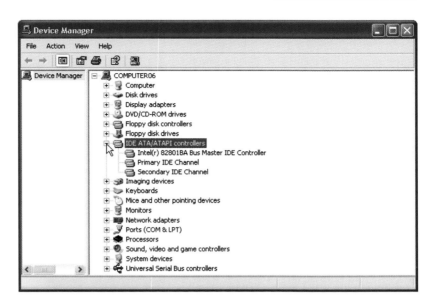

In the *Hardware* tab, click *Device Manager*. Afterwards, open the category *IDE ATA/ ATAPI* by double-clicking it.

Double-click *Primary IDE channel* and switch to the advanced setting in the next dialog window.

You can see both drives, which are connected to or which can be connected to the controller. Under *Transfer Mode*, *select* the option *DMA if available*. If the *Current Transfer Mode* is set to *Ultra DMA Mode*, you can be sure that the device will choose the fastest possible way. If the settings *PIO Only* and *DMA if available* are displayed, however, you can act on the assumption that you are using an outdated device that is slowing your system down.

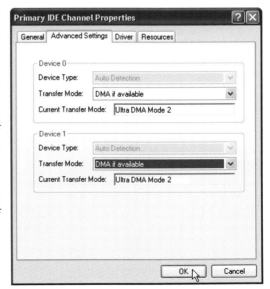

9. Preparing your system for video editing

Think about getting a new hard disk ...

Now, check your secondary IDE channel.

DirectX

DirectX provides the required driver to edit videos in Windows on your computer. In addition, most games and multimedia applications use DirectX, in particular to control fast 3D graphics, for instance. It is also important always to use the newest version of DirectX when video editing – even if it might be a nuisance to, for instance, download the rather big file from the Internet. Some software might not run at all without it!

You can check easily whether DirectX is working properly on your computer:

1 Select *Run* from the *Start* menu and enter DXDIAG. Click *OK*.

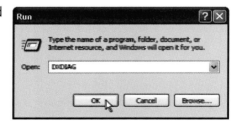

2 After a few seconds, the DirectX Diagnostic Tool opens. By means of the different tabs, you can check whether all of your DirectX drivers work properly.

3 Switch to the DirectX Files tab. From the *Notes* section you can determine that no problems have been found.

Check all of the other tabs as well. The device driver might cause any problems displayed on the other tabs. XP might have not recognized your graphics card, or you might be using an outdated driver.

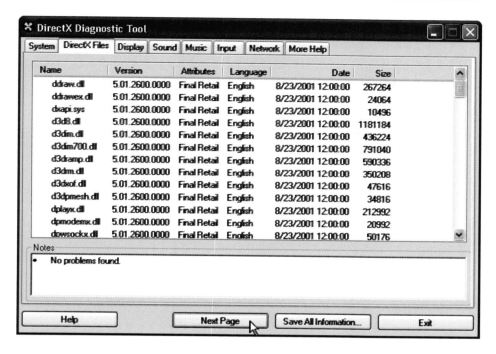

As a starting point to solve a problem, go to *Help and Support* in the *Start* menu. Click *Tools* and select the entry My Computer Information from the list on the left. Afterwards, click *View the status of system hardware and software*. A problem report is created, and links you to different Help sites.

In Windows XP, you are unlikely to run into problems with DirectX as long as you are using a current graphics card. During the installation, the drivers that were certified by Windows are installed automatically.

No useless programs in the background

All applications running in the background should be closed because they will affect your computer's performance in a negative way. This applies particularly to caching programs such as *FastFind*, for instance, which is automatically installed with Microsoft Word. It is the task of caching programs to reduce the number of times your hard disk is accessed by storing frequently used data in RAM. If the

141

system needs the data, it can directly access it from the virtual memory. This is at first not a problem during the digitization process because, initially, data is not read but only written to the hard disk. Problems arise quickly, however, if cache applications are working in write-behind mode. In this mode, data is only written to the hard disk when the processor is not busy – which is exactly the case during the digitizing process.

In addition, turn off your screen saver, virus scanner, and your Firewall (if installed). The latter intervenes as soon as data is written to your hard disk.

No power management is required during the digitization process. Because of its negative effects on the system performance, you should turn it off as well.

Be careful when working on a network

Are you working on a network? If so, you should disable the accessing of your hard disk for reading and writing purposes during the digitization period.

In Explorer, right-click the folders that have been shared and select *Sharing and Security*.

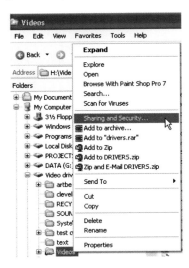

In the next dialog window, select *Do not share this folder*.

Your computer is now optimized for capturing your video; you can start the recording process.

The correct video card

Theoretically, a simple FireWire card should be sufficient to cut your videos. However, camcorders are not particularly intelligent – and neither is the FireWire card. If the data is not supplied and removed fast enough, images might be missing. Consequently, the recording of your video might be interrupted, or your video might contain unsightly gaps later on. In addition, the software has to support the control system of your camera – and it has to do that at the correct time.

All in all, it sounds like a pretty problematic undertaking, which is, however, usually successful with Windows XP and the smart editing programs available nowadays – but things don't always run smoothly. Very often, it depends on a number of additional factors such as the motherboard of your PC or its chip set.

143

9. Preparing your system for video editing

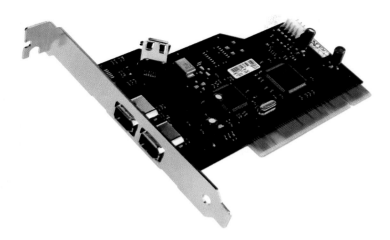

Proper DV capture cards attach to interfaces that were specifically developed for video applications and can separate the control code from the data material. This way, they can take over the camera controls, and compatibility problems are avoided. Even an interruption of the data flow (whether it is caused by the hard disk or the PCI bus) while such a card is used does not pose a problem because the data is temporarily buffered.

With some practice, however, you can use your simple FireWire card to cut your videos without foregoing professional features.

The FireWire card is actually not a video capture card; it is an interface for your computer. That's the reason why many of these cards have an internal connection as well to which FireWire hard disks can be connected, for instance. The FireWire standard made video editing on PCs affordable for the bulk of the population because there is no need to use a special video card.

Configuring the video capture card

After you have installed the FireWire card in your computer and started Windows XP, the installation will be started automatically. You will only receive a message notifying you that a FireWire card has been found in your system, and that the drivers will now be installed.

Following this installation, you can already start the recording of your video. All you still have to do is connect the camcorder to your PC with the cable provided. It doesn't matter which jack you use on the FireWire card.

> **FireWire card under Windows 98 SE and Windows 2000**
>
> Windows 98SE: Digital video editing by using a FireWire card has only been possible since the second edition of Windows 98. After the FireWire card has been installed and Windows restarted, you must keep the Windows CD ready. The hardware wizard alerts you that a card was found and guides you through the installation. Just select a driver that the wizard makes available to you.
>
> Windows 2000: As long as Service Pack 1 has been installed, you should not have any problems with the installation. Windows automatically provides you with a list of possible drivers from which you must choose the Microsoft driver.

Installing analog capture cards

If you want to use an analog capture card, you must pay close attention to the sequence of installation steps. It is essential that you refer to the manual of the card to find out whether the card or the driver has to be installed first. Usually, the driver of the card has to be installed before the card.

Before you install the driver, you should take the trouble and visit the manufacturer's Web site as there might be a more up-to date driver available. Video cards can lie on the dealer's shelves for quite some time; and therefore it might very well be that a newer version of the software has become available in the meantime.

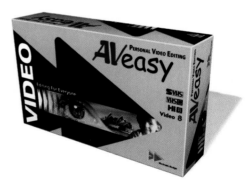

Tips for creating professional-looking movies

To avoid problems during the actual filming of your videos, keep these basic rules in mind:

- You should familiarize yourself with the functions of your camcorder and always take the camcorder's manual with you when you are shooting a video. You never know what weather conditions you might encounter. The camcorder offers many functions that you can use to optimally adjust the camera to the surrounding area.

- A set of charged backup batteries is a must. You might not always have the opportunity to recharge your used-up batteries. Just imagine missing that outstanding scene because your batteries are running out. Backup batteries are not cheap, but without them you might squander the enjoyment of filming because you worry if the batteries will last you through the day.

- Keep an adequate supply of tapes at hand and shoot as much as you want. Don't hold back. You can decide what scenes to keep in the video later on, when you actually cut it. It would be a tremendous regret if a shot were missing when you tried to portray the situation to other viewers later on.

- If you are panning shots, include a still scene of about 20 seconds at the beginning and end of the panning. If you don't have a tripod handy, place your camcorder on an even surface such as the roof of a car or a wall. Place a piece of fabric or a newspaper underneath your camera to protect it from scratches. This way, it is also easier to pan with the camcorder.

- Refrain from zooming too much because it often appears confusing rather than aesthetic. If you zoom, shoot a couple of normal scenes afterwards. When you are editing the video on your PC afterwards, you can always obtain the same effect by using the appropriate transitions of your video editing software without drawing the viewer's attention to confusing zoom movements.

146

Camera position (views):

- Long shot: Provides an overall overview about the events happening in front of the lens. More importance is attached to the entire room than to the individual objects in it. This camera view provides a lot of information and the human eye might need a certain amount of time to become familiar with it. You should not use this view to often.

- Semi-long shot: The same importance is attached to objects in front of the camera as well as the surrounding area. This position allows for a better resolution of details than the long shot.

- Medium shot: This camera position focuses even more on the shot objects. If you are shooting people, the bottom edge of the video image is just below the belly button whereby the movement of arms is still recorded. This camera position is suitable for a maximum of two people (as often seen in talk shows).

- Medium close-up: The face and upper part of the body of *one* person come into foreground. The bottom edge of the video image is located around the person's chest.

- Close-up: In this camera position, you concentrate on a person's face. The shot range lies between the forehead and chin. Consequently, the viewer is brought close to the person being filmed.

- Extreme close-up: This camera position attracts attention to a single detail such as the mouth, for instance. The filmed object is brought extremely close to the viewer. For this reason, you should use this camera position sparingly.

- Camera height: If possible, the camera should be positioned at eye level or adjusted to the object's height. If the camera is placed too low, objects might dominate and overwhelm the viewer if the camera is too high, objects might appear strange.

Glossary

Animation

Usually refers to cartoons that were created with special computer programs

AVI

Audio Video Interleaved. Simple but popular standard format for video clip files. Video and audio files are saved within one file. AVI files use different codecs.

Bitmap

A special image format for computers. In bitmap format, images are made up of individual dots, the pixels.

Bit rate

The number of bits that pass a given point in a telecommunication network in a given amount of time, usually a second. The higher the bit rate, the better the quality of the video.

Capture

Digitizing clip short video codec; Algorithm for the →compression and →decompression Decompression Restoration of compressed data. The →codec decompresses the compressed →AVI files and makes them available to the video hardware of the computer in a useable format.

Camcorder

A combination of camera and recorder

Chrominance

Color component of a video signal

Codec

An abbreviation for COmpressor/DECompressor. It describes a software driver that controls the compression during the capture of the video and the decompression during its playback. Extensive algorithms are behind it.

Color Sampling

A compression process that reduces the color components of a video but simultaneously maintains the information about luminosity

Decompression

Restoration of compressed data. The →codec decompresses the compressed →AVI data and provides it to the video hardware of the computer in a usable format.

Delta frame

A single frame of which only the difference to the preceding →key frame is saved. Therefore it cannot stand on its own. Delta frames are not supported by every →codec.

Desktop Video

Using a PC for the video editing process

DirectX

A technology developed by Windows that allows for an accelerated playback of moving images in Windows – as is the case with videos or games. The programs directly access the memory of the graphics card and consequently relieve the processor.

Dropout

The loss of images because of videotapes that are in less than perfect condition or because of bad data transfer.

Glossary

fps

This is a unit for the playback speed of videos: *frames per second*. The common rate in the USA is 30 fps. In Europe, it is 25 fps.

Frame

Single image

Frame grabber

Video card used for digitizing video signals

Key frame

A single image (reference frame) that contains all of the data (in comparison to delta frames) and on which delta frames are based

FireWire

A term introduced by Apple referring to the IEEE-1394 interface. Data from digital video devices is transferred via this interface.

Compression

Reduction of the file size: Loss-free compression: All of the data remains; only the type of coding is modified (such as ZIP files, for instance). Lossy compression: Unimportant data is more or less disregarded. The criteria depends on the codec

Luminance

Luminance component of a video signal

Motion effect

The term "motion effect" refers to a change in playback speed: slow motion, fast forward, as well as strobe effect (stroboscope effect)

MJPEG

A file format that is usually hardware-based: MotionJPEG is a further development of the JPEG standard for graphic files.

MPEG

A file format defined by the Motion Pictures Experts Group with extensive algorithms and strong compression. Because of the high processing effort, it was reasonable to use only a hardware-based implementation for a long time.

NTSC

North American TV standard. Videos and broadcasts in this standard cannot be played back on PAL devices.

PAL

European TV standard. Videos in this format cannot be played back on NTSC devices.

QuickTime

An alternative to Windows AVI format, which was developed by Apple. QuickTime movies can be played back on a PC as well as on Macintosh. QuickTime must be installed for this purpose.

Streaming

Transmitting videos through the Internet or other networks. Not all of the data has to be downloaded before playing back the movie – the remaining data is automatically downloaded in the background.

S-Video

Abbreviation for *Super-Video*. A technology used to playback a video at its best possible quality. The video is separated in its luminance and chrominance components, which are transferred separately.

Index

Index

Notes

Check out all of our *Fast Bytes* books!
Only $12.95 each!

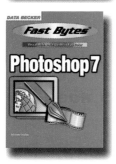

www.databecker.com

Notes